AF433330

BESSIE COLEMAN
America's first licensed Negro pilot

BLACK WINGS

LIEUT. WILLIAM J. POWELL

1934

IVAN DEACH, JR.
Publisher . . . Los Angeles

DEDICATION

To the memory of Bessie Coleman, the first Negro to fly an aeroplane successfully, who, although possessed of all the feminine charms that man admires in the opposite sex, also displayed courage equal to that of the most daring men, this volume is humbly dedicated.

Writing the introductory paragraphs to such a book as this is similar to reporting the events of a World's Fair—having secured one's information by looking through the keyhole of the administration building.

To give even an epitome of the life, the struggles, the sacrifices and ambitions of the author would require more space than can here be utilized. To catch the burning vision of Lieutenant Powell is but to know him. Like most great pioneers and men of vision he has been misunderstood by those who should have aided him. The temper of steel, however, can best be determined by refining—the character of man is best realized in the presence of the heat of misunderstanding and cynicism. In Powell's heart there is no bitterness. His all-consuming dream of filling the sky with skilled *black wings* has kept him lofty of ideals, big of spirit, and free of mind.

To the vast host of surging black feet which now are beating a faint tattoo on the horizon of America, this book should be of invaluable service.

To those of all races who are moved by the courage and skill of men who dare to do, in spite of all opposition, this story should provide a source of encouragement and inspiration.

To the Negro youth who believes or imagines that the proverbial American "color line" is an insurmountable barrier, this book should be a never-failing compass pointing toward those places where men of will *will* win! And for those interested in the technique and science of aviation—black or white—this story should prove instructive reading.

It is obvious that Lieutenant Powell has been for

some time cognizant of the limitations of Negroes in industry, recently cited in a chapter of *Brown America*, by Edwin R. Embree, who states: "Even though Negroes have taken up a number of trades and industries in the northern cities in which previously they were meagerly represented, they are still a step or two behind the procession. . . . . Into such expanding specialties as *radio* and *aeronautics, Negroes have found but little place.*"

On the other hand the author is guided by the belief that what Negroes have done in other fields can be done—*must* be done—in aviation.

The pages of history, to the careful reader, are replete with stories of pioneering and martyrdom.

"Many Negroes came in the rush of the 'forty-niners' as pioneers and miners as well as slaves." . . . "William Alexander Leidsroff was the most distinguished Negro pioneer of California and at one time lived in the largest house in San Francisco. He owned the first steamship sailing in San Francisco Bay, and was a prominent business man, a member of the City Council and treasurer and member of the school committee . . . ."

"The Negro's work as a pioneer extends down until our day. The late Commodore Peary who discovered the North Pole said: 'Matthew A. Henson, my Negro assistant, has been with me in one capacity or another since my second trip to Nicaragua in 1887. I have taken him on each and all of my expeditions, except the first, and also without exception on each of my farthest sledge trips. This position I have given him primarily because of his adaptability and fitness for the work, and secondly on account of his loyalty . . .' This leaves Henson to-day as the only living human being who has stood at the North Pole."*

**The Gift of Black Folk*, by W. E. B. DuBois (Chap. I, pp. 50-51).

The dedication of this book bespeaks the niche which Negroes have carved in the rugged death list of aviation heroes. That a black transcontinental flyer sleeps beneath the sod will be, no doubt, startling information to many readers. This and other facts contained herein will be comforting evidence to those who await the fulfillment of the Psalmist's prophecy: "Princes shall come out of Egypt, Ethiopia shall soon stretch out her hands unto God." A paraphrase of the lines of Georgia Douglass Johnson is, I believe, symbolical of the philosophy and dreams of Lieutenant William J. Powell and those linking hands and hearts with him:

> "We are the Black Flyers
> We're awake, we're away!
> We have jewels in trust
> They are rights of the soul,
> That are noble and just.
> There are deeds to be done
> There are goals to be won
> We're stripped for the race
> In the glare of the sun,
> We're throbbing with faith
> We can and we must.
> *Our Black Wings pointed toward God*
> *Must not trail in the dust."*

FLOYD C. COVINGTON
Executive Secretary
Los Angeles Urban League

CONTENTS

ILLUSTRATIONS

From the beginning of time, man's greatest ambition has been to annihilate time and space. This ambition has led to the development of all the great industries, the greatest of which are the shipping industry, the railroad industry, the automobile industry, and the radio industry. In these industries, as in all others, the pioneers, or those who got in on the "ground floor" and helped lay the cornerstone, are the ones who were made wealthy.

Unfortunately, American Negroes, for various reasons, have not pioneered in any of these industries, and, instead of becoming producers, have been nearly one hundred per cent consumers, having to make themselves content with the menial, low-paying jobs that others see fit to give them, becoming wholly dependent, therefore, upon others for the very essentials of life itself.

Through this lack of initiative, not only have we become dependent upon other races for existence, but even now as this book goes to press, we are actually being replaced in all lines of work by Japanese, Filipinos, Mexicans, Chinese, and in many instances by whites, thus placing the Negro in a very critical predicament. Our own leaders are not facing the facts as they really are, and our friends of the white race do not touch the subject at all.

As an illustration of this lack of initiative, I have a friend in Los Angeles who has been chauffeur for a prominent movie actor for the last eight years. One day his employer said to him: "Joe, I am going to send you to an aviation school next month in order that you may learn to fly an airplane . . . . ." but before he finished his statement, Joe interrupted:

"Oh, no, Boss, not me! I'm afraid to go up in a plane. I'll never fly unless aeroplanes start to fly on the ground."

"But, yes," insisted the employer, "I've ordered an airplane already, and have made arrangements for you to get your training."

Several times after that, he tried to talk Joe into the idea of learning to fly, but he absolutely could not convince him. One morning, about a month later, when Joe was in the kitchen talking to the colored cook, his employer walked in and handed him a check.

"What's this?" asked Joe, surprised.

"I'm sorry, Joe," said the employer. "You're a very conscientious worker and we all like you, but I've bought an airplane and have hired a man for chauffeur who can pilot the plane also. You see, Joe, I can't afford two men. My chauffeur must be able to drive me to the field, park the car, fly me to my destination and return, and then jump into the automobile and drive me back to the office. I tried every way I knew to get you to take a flying course in order that you might retain your job, but you refused."

Joe was stunned. One could see the blood leaving his face, even as dark as he is. He could not say a word. Just to think—he had worked faithfully on the job for the last eight years. He thought nothing could cause his employer to discharge him. But he did not reckon with the fact that to live nowadays, one must make himself fit in every manner possible.

Now Joe is one of aviation's greatest enthusiasts. He has been trying to get a course ever since, but now is out of a job and has no money. He let his one big opportunity pass him by.

Joe represents thousands of Negro chauffeurs throughout America. The white man has always considered the Negro the logical servant to drive him around . . . . even in the days of the horse and buggy and the hack. Now that the white man is advancing rapidly toward the constant use of the airplane, *is the Negro to pass out of the picture in this line of employ? He will unless he learns aviation now.* I trust this book will serve as an inspiration to the thousands of Negro chauffers in America.

THE AUTHOR, LIEUT. WILLIAM J. POWELL
Instructor, Aeronautics, Jefferson Evening High School, Los Angeles

This book is written to stimulate interest among Negroes in a new industry, aviation, which is destined to become the most gigantic of all industries, though still in its pioneer stages. It is a true story of the struggles of a few young Negroes bent on stirring up general interest in aviation among Negroes throughout America. There is a better job and a better future in aviation for Negroes than in any other industry, and the reason is this: *aviation is just beginning its period of growth and if we get into it now, while it is still uncrowded, we can grow as aviation grows.*

Very soon air travel will be as common as railroad transportation is to-day. Many of my readers will not accept this statement, but if they will acquaint themselves with statistics on the development of the transportation industries they will readily agree with me.

I trust my story may produce a picture that will arouse the interest of the Negro in flying—that he will wake up to his opportunities and not let "the other man start traveling by radio, before he starts traveling by airplane."

I trust also that my story may show the Negro schoolboy and girl a wide open field of industry, full of opportunities leading to fame and fortune, in which there is still a chance for the Negro to reach the highest pinnacles even in production and distribution.

Again, I trust my story may bring the Negro business man and the Negro financier to realize that untold wealth lies in the development of passenger and freight air service, and that they may realize that if the Negro expects to ride below the Mason and Dixon line as a free man should ride, he must ride in an airplane owned and operated by Negroes.

Stimulating interest in aviation among Negroes would not be such an arduous task were it not for stumbling blocks which seriously menace the Negro's entry into any line of commercial endeavor. Skepticism, superstition, mistrust, jealousy, lack of co-operation, lack of preparation, race prejudice, and lack of finance have caused many a young Negro to turn away from some field of commercial endeavor with disgust. These form the basis for my story, and I trust and sincerely hope that this book will serve as a guide to those of my race whose ambition it is to become the flyers of the future, in order that they may know what to expect and be ready for it.

Some of my readers may think me rather harsh for my true presentation of these matters, and my criticisms of the various flyers, but I offer no apology, because this book is written to serve as a guide and inspiration for the future Negro flyers, and in the interest of the advancement of aviation among Negroes. I feel sure that, with the good of our race at heart, not even those mentioned in the pages of this book will object to my pointing out the facts, in order that future Negro flyers will benefit therefrom.

We have lost money, we have bought airplanes, we have flown them, we have cracked them up, and we're flying them some more, for the job must be done. No one is making us do it. We are flying of our own free will and accord, for *the conquest of the air is an accomplished fact.*

In closing I wish to express my sincere appreciation to all of those—of both races—who, through their assistance and inspiration, have enabled this little band of Negro air enthusiasts to carry on. To mention all of their names would mean increasing the size of this book many pages, but a few I shall mention. First, of course, must come Major William S. Braddan, Chaplain of the famous Eighth Infantry, Illinois National Guard, whose wager made possible the plot; to Burrell Neely, who played a great part in laying the foundation for this story; Mr. Floyd C. Covington, Executive Secretary of the Los Angeles Branch of the Urban League, who suggested the name for the book; Congressman Oscar Depriest, who furnished the statistical information in the Appendix, and whose support has been very helpful; Rev. J. C. Austin, Pastor of the Pilgrim Baptist Church, Chicago, whose speeches on behalf of aviation have stirred up much interest; my present spiritual advisor, Rev. J. A. H. Eldridge, Pastor of the Beth Eden Temple, Los Angeles; Mrs. Eva Burton, President of the Chicago Club, Pasadena, California; Robert L. Vann, Editor of the Pittsburgh Courier, whose releases on Negro progress in aviation have probably been the Negro's greatest stimulus in flying; David Eugene Taylor, Editor of the California News, Los Angeles, whose columns have always kept the West Coast readers informed of our progress in aviation; and Mr. and Mrs. Fred D. Grant and Mr. and Mrs. Woody Washington of Santa Monica, California.

WILLIAM J. POWELL.

LIEUT. COL. WILLIAM S. BRADDAN
Chaplain, 8th Infantry, Illinois National Guard

CHAPTER I

BILL'S FIRST AIRPLANE RIDE

It was a hot afternoon in August, 1927, when, after mopping the perspiration from their faces and flinging themselves across the beds exhausted, Major William S. Braddan said to Bill Brown—"Bill, I don't think I'll go with you to the airport tomorrow. Eight hours of marching makes me a fit subject for rest." Braddan's declaration drew no argument from Bill, for he also had marched eight hours down the avenue des Champs Élysées, the long boulevard des Capucines, and des Italiens, over the avenue de L'Opera and the rue de la Paix. This eight hour march was the feature of the American Legion Convention in Paris, France, where Major Braddan and Bill went as delegates from the George L. Giles Post in Chicago.

So elated were they while marching through the beautiful Parisian streets, thronged with millions of French people, that they did not realize how exhausted they were until they lay down. In a few seconds they were fast asleep, thus eliminating the usual debate as to where they would go on the morrow. Up to this time Major Braddan and Bill had always been together while visiting the places of interest in France, Braddan acting as a wonderful father to Bill, always advising him not to "step out" too far.

The next morning Bill was up bright and early, a good night's rest being all that was necessary to rid him of the strains of exhaustion caused by eight hours of marching the previous day. He was still a young man, just past his twenty-eighth birthday a month previous. Not so with the Reverend, however. I say Reverend, for besides being the Chaplain of the famous

Eighth Infantry, Illinois National Guard, holding the rank of Major, Braddan was also Pastor of the Berean Baptist Church, one of the leading churches of Chicago, of which Bill was a member. Braddan admonished Bill several times not to call him "Reverend", however, while in France, but "Major" instead.

"No, Bill, I think I had better stay in today. I haven't completely recovered from that march yet. Anyhow, I have a hunch that you might get into something today that I do not care to take part in. I'll stay in and rest. Have a good time."

Yes, he did have a hunch. He knew Bill planned to take an airplane ride over Paris. Was he afraid to go up? Surely not. A minister certainly was not afraid to take an airplane ride.

In a jiffy, Bill was in an automobile bound for the American Legion headquarters. Standing in front of the headquarters, Bill ran into Burrell Neely, a

BILL AT VERSAILLES, FRANCE

delegate from Wichita, Kansas. He had only known Neely for a few days, but soon learned that he was in for 'most anything, that he was very alert and quite progressive.

"Neely, want to take a ride out to Le Bourget Field?" inquired Bill. "Sure thing, Pal", Neely replied, and soon both were speeding in the direction of the air field where Colonel Charles Lindbergh had landed just four months previous on his epochal flight across the ocean.

Lindbergh's flight had made Le Bourget Field a

place of great interest to the American Legionnaires, and it is safe to estimate that a large majority of the 30,000 visiting Americans paid homage to that great American by taking a ride at this field. Bill had never been up, neither had Neely. Plane after plane rose majestically from the ground, faded into the distance, and returned, discharging its passengers, men, women and children. Neither of them, however, had mustered enough courage to say, "Let's go up."

Suddenly a large crowd at the south end of the field attracted everyone's attention. Bill and Neely ran over, and, to their great surprise, saw several Frenchmen trying to get a large cow up a gangplank into an airplane. Then a young Frenchman came along with a large box containing two large chickens. They were placed in the airplane, the plank lowered, the door closed, and soon the big machine rose into the air with the cow and the chickens. Neely's mouth was wide open and Bill's eyes were fixed on the plane as it soon faded from view. After getting over their surprise, Bill, who had a fairly good knowledge of the French language, ascertained that the cow and chickens had to be rushed to the stock show in London for exhibition that afternoon, and of course the only way to get them there in time was to take them by air.

Neely looked at Bill. Bill looked at Neely. They exchanged speechless messages. Neely broke the silence and said, "Even the cows and chickens, women and children are riding in airplanes and here we are, supposed to be men, afraid to go up." Not another word was necessary. You could not tell a World War Veteran that he was afraid of anything and get away with it. Before the boys realized what they were doing, they had purchased tickets and found themselves seated in the large passenger plane for a ride over Paris.

The big motors began to speed up, fast, faster, but not as fast as these boys' hearts began to beat. Perspiration began to pop out on Bill's forehead. He was about to take off on his first airplane ride. All kinds of thoughts passed through his mind. Would he land safely? Would he get air-sick as many had told him he would? Would the plane fall? Probably it would be all right going up but what about coming down? He was sure he would die coming down because he could not stand to come down on a fast elevator—it always seemed as if his stomach was going up to meet his palate. Why had he been so foolish? Certainly this would be the end of him. Across the aisle sat Neely. His legs were spread out and his hands clutched the seat in front of him as though he was bracing himself for a terrible shakeup. His large white eyes rolled over in Bill's direction. He was scared stiff. It was so noticeable that Bill began to look about at the rest of the passengers, and felt quite ashamed as he glanced ahead and saw others including three women and a small boy of about seven calmly laughing and talking.

But now the plane is moving. A rumble, bump, bump, thump, along the ground. A few more rumbles and thumps and presently the rumbles cease. Why, they were up in the air! How surprised they were. They did not even know when they left the ground because both of them had had their eyes closed tightly. They marvelled how smoothly the plane now seemed to move. At times it did not even seem to be moving— just seemed to be floating out in space. Soon they were passing over the Seine river. The scenery was beautiful. Unconsciously, Neely let go his death hold on the seat in front of him. He pointed to the Eiffel Tower. How magnificent Paris is from the air! They could recognize la place de la Concorde. The great cathedral of Paris, Notre Dame, is discernible. How foolish our boys were. They had never experienced a more pleasant ride. It was smoother by far than a ride on a Pullman train, or even on an ocean liner.

But maybe the worst was yet to come, each thought. They had to land. The noise of the motors ceased. Each grasped the seat in front of him again. The nose of the ship pointed downward. Again many silly thoughts speeded through their minds. Again perspiration began to break out on Bill's forehead. But before either of them had come to himself the plane had stopped and the passengers were unloading. They were the last to leave the plane.

"So we are down," said Neely, "and you couldn't even tell we were coming down. My, how some people can lie. Riding in an airplane is nothing like some have told me it was. Say, I could go to sleep up there."

"Yes," said Bill, "I'm thinking that those who tell the terrible tales about getting sick, etc., from an airplane ride have never been up. Let's go up again."

And thus began something that the boys have never been able to finish. Bill had completed his first airplane ride. That ride was to lead to many adventures. That ride was the turning point in Bill's life.

They watched the planes for at least two more hours. They marvelled at the number of passengers who arrived at various intervals and purchased tickets to London, Brussels, Marseilles, Nice, and other points of destination. It was nothing new to these people, and they carried their hand grips along just as they would when taking a ride on a train.

For a long time both the boys were silent, when Bill said: "Commercial aviation seems to be much more advanced over here than it is in America, don't you think, Neely? But, you know Uncle Sam never lags behind in the development of an important industry. From what I see here, I predict that in a few years, which probably will be in my time and yours, air travel will be as common as any other mode of transportation. I foresee more airplanes in the air than automobiles on the ground, for there is more space up there. That brings an idea to mind. What of the Negro? Neely, do you realize that Negroes in America have never pioneered in any of the large industries, and that is the reason we have no leaders in any of them? The automobile, the radio, the moving picture, and all other large industries have grown from nothing to gigantic industries; they all have produced thousands of millionaires and millions of good paying jobs, all of which have passed the Negro by. But this wealth and these good jobs have rightfully gone to those who dared pioneer the trail. I haven't heard of a single Negro in America who got in on the ground floor of any large industry, and what is the result? We have had to content ourselves with the menial low-paying jobs that the other man saw fit to give us. Thousands of our young men and women are graduating from college, but, after college, then what? As a race we have neither factories nor commercial houses to absorb the growing number of graduates. But it is our duty to put forth every effort to find a more lucrative field for these young men and women who have been trained to think for themselves, and an opening should be found for them before necessity compels them to use their talents in the wrong direction. Street corners, pool rooms, lottery houses and the like furnish no outlet for the ability of a college man, but I now see unlimited possibilities in aviation. Neely, there is before our very eyes an infant industry that some day bids fair to become a bigger giant than any. We have an opportunity to get in on the ground floor, an opportunity to help develop this industry—we have an opportunity to grow with this industry, an opportunity to become producers—what shall we do?"

"Wonderful, wonderful thought, Bill", replied Neely. "And any progressive, far-sighted person can readily see a bright future in aviation. Yes, people are going to fly, people *are* flying; and the Negro can do everything that everyone else does, so it is only logi-

cal that he will fly too. But, will he start now, or will
he wait until the industry is completely monopolized;
will he content himself with jobs as grease monkeys,
airplane washers and polishers, etc., or will he jump
into it now and learn to design, manufacture, and distribute airplanes and their accessories?"

Bill broke in again: "It would be a great thing to
get our people to get into aviation on a large scale, but
I guess it will be a terrible job to educate our folks
to the use of the airplane. You know the old expression whenever anyone suggests an airplane ride, they
say, 'Yes, providing they can keep one foot on the
ground.'—I suppose it will take many a flying demonstration, many a lecture and whatnot to override
this feeling in our masses."

"Oh, it shouldn't be such a task", replied Neely.
"The whites are taking right to it."

"But the whites are born pioneers, and are constantly searching for something new," sighed Bill.
"On the other hand we don't take up a thing until it is
generally accepted as O. K."

"And then we usually run it into the ground", in-
jected Neely laughing. "Then, too, Negroes in general
haven't enough money to buy airplanes. Do you think
there will ever be a potential market in our race in
the airplane industry?" Neely continued.

"Say, feller", said Bill a little angered, "you know
a colored man always manages to get just about what
he wants. The great trouble is they don't want much.
Everyone said colored people didn't have money
enough to buy automobiles, but what do we find? We
find them owning all kinds of cars, the majority even
owning an automobile before owning a home, and
after they learn to like it, they will be the same way
about airplanes. I actually believe that with the proper
leadership, Negroes can be systematically trained to
the use of the airplane to such an extent that a great
airplane industry might spring up with Negroes de-

signing, manufacturing, distributing, selling airplanes, out of which would come well-regulated air lines with colored pilots, mechanics, radio men, airport managers, and everything. You know transportation is one of the greatest factors of human progress."

Neely sighed and said, "Say, Pal, the more we talk about this thing the bigger it gets. It would be a wonderful thing to connect all Southern cities with airlines owned and operated by Negroes, so that we wouldn't have to be disgraced by having to ride a Jim Crow train or bus; and then all the thousands of dollars spent daily by our people on railroads and busses would be diverted back into our own race. What an idea."

And as the two talked they walked into one of the large hangars to inspect the planes there. Suddenly Neely grasped Bill's arm and said, "Really, Bill, do you intend to go back to the States and take up aviation?"

"Yes, sir, I have made up my mind," replied Bill. "Are you with me?"

"But neither of us knows the first thing about aviation."

"True, but we can learn like others have done."

Neely pondered awhile and then said, "Well, Pal, I read in a magazine that for every man up in the air it required nine men on the ground. You be the one up in the air and I'll be the nine on the ground. I'll handle the business. You know I am business manager of the Negro Star, the only Negro newspaper in the state of Kansas, and, while I think of it, give me your address in Chicago, and I'll see that you get on our mailing list when I return."

Neely was quite serious about the new venture, and, although he did not care to become a flyer, he really thought he could be the equivalent of the nine men on the ground.

The boys made a bargain with each other, Bill declaring that he would enter an aviation school as soon as he returned to the United States, and Neely would join him when he finished, to act as business manager of the proposed aviation venture. After a hearty handshake to bind the deal, they resumed their inspection of the planes.

Presently a very cheerful and polite Frenchman accosted them. *"Bon jour, messieurs"*, said he.

"Bon jour, monsieur," replied Bill.

"Desirez-vous un voyage par air?" he queried.

"Merci, monsieur, mais nous avons déjà monté le haut, aujourd'hui," replied Bill, hoping he had spoken correctly, and trying to get away from the Frenchman.

But the Frenchman started again—*"Bon! Desirez-vous apprendre voler?"*

STUDENTS—FRENCH AVIATION SCHOOL

"What's he saying?" said Neely.

"Oh, he asked me if we wanted to take a ride and I told him we had already been up today. Now he wants to know if we want to learn to fly."

"Wee, wee," said Neely, elated, flopping his arms like a bird at the Frenchman. "Tell him yes, Bill."

So, after quite a conversation in which Bill had difficulty in recalling all the French he had learned at the University of Illinois (as it seemed he must recall all of it to talk to this Frenchman) he felt happy to know that they were made welcome to the first aviation school they had visited. The Frenchman almost insisted that Bill return to Paris and enter his school of aviation. To let him tell it, there was not a better school of aviation in the world and his price was "le moins cher" (cheapest) of all. He showed the boys all through the various departments, which were wonderfully equipped with the very latest facilities.

"I would like to attend that French school," said Bill on their way home, "but I am afraid that my knowledge of the French language is too limited. I would be confronted with the task of learning the new terms first in English and then in French, which would be double work."

"Bill, I think you should attend this school, as the prestige gained will be a wonderful boost for us to start. Think of it: 'Aviator Bill Brown, graduate of the Paris School of Aviation.' There is no other choice for you," said Neely.

"Yes, there is," Bill replied. "After all, there's no place like the good old U. S. A."

"Oh, yeah?" Neely interrupted, "I hope you will always feel that way."

"Say, Neely, there's sarcasm in that statement— what do you mean?"

"Oh nothing, Pal, I only hope you'll always think the same way, that's all."

What did he mean? By this time Bill had learned that Neely was a deep thinker, although comical at times, and it was well seriously to consider his serious statements. Such a statement coming from one who was as patriotic as Neely, who volunteered his services during the World War, caused Bill to be a little bit disturbed.

CHAPTER II

IN DESPAIR

"So long, Pal, good luck. Sorry I'm not going back on your ship so we could discuss our plans further, but on my way to Wichita I'll stop off in Chicago and pay you a visit. Pleasant voyage, Major."

These were Neely's last words on the wharf at Le Havre, France, as Major Braddan and Bill Brown strode up the long gangplank to the Ile de France for their return trip to the United States. Yes, Bill was sorry, too, that Neely's reservation was on the Leviathan, which sailed from this same port one week later, for the restful sea journey back to the States seemed to sharpen Bill's thinking capacities, causing many a bright idea for the future aviation adventure to be ever forthcoming, only to be dampened by the objections of Major Braddan, who never agreed with Bill's idea of giving up his business in Chicago for aviation.

"No, Bill", said Braddan the next day as they reclined in the large comfortable deck chairs enjoying the sunshine and the fresh salt air from the ocean, "I wouldn't do it. You are foolish. You have a good business. You have had sixteen on your payroll now for five years. You have a wonderful business. Never swap horses in the middle of the stream. This aviation is a new thing, and you know our people do not take to new things readily, and, believe you me, you'll regret many a time that you made the change."

"Well, Reverend Braddan," said Bill, "you don't understand. My business has been on the decline for the past year and a half. So many garages and filling stations have sprung up near me that I have been entertaining the idea of selling for the last six months.

Anyway, our people should wake up to the aviation industry now, not next year nor the following year, but *now*, while they have the great opportunity to become producers. That's what's prompting me."

Just then, Florence Mills, who was returning to New York aboard the same ship, approached.

"Say, doesn't she look hot, Reverend," said Bill, sitting up straight in the chair.

"I'll say she does", replied Braddan, also sitting up.

The charming young lady spoke—"Good morning, Major Braddan. Isn't this air wonderful? I could stay on an ocean liner forever. I get such a wonderful appetite that I always gain several pounds crossing."

By this time the boys were standing.

"I believe you gained a few pounds at the dinner given by Glover Compton last week, too. I never saw a little woman enjoy eating so much," said Braddan, laughing.

"Yes", she replied. "Nettie Compton is such a wonderful cook, and it had been so long since I'd had any real American home cooking, that I just tried to eat everything. Weren't those rolls delicious? You know, Major, since I have been abroad, I have dined in some of the most fashionable cafes and hotels in Paris, London, Berlin, Vienna, and other places, but don't you know I have never run across a cook that could equal our colored mothers at home."

"Pardon me," interrupted Braddan. "Mr. Brown, this is little Florence Mills."

"How do you do, Miss Mills. We are fortunate indeed to be on board with such celebrities as yourself and Mayor Jimmy Walker," Bill said, smiling.

"Oh", she said shyly, "Mayor Jimmy Walker is returning to New York on this ship. We are indeed fortunate. They say that is the reason this ship is making such wonderful time. The Captain told me we are expected to make the trip in five days flat."

Braddan interrupted again—"Bill was invited over

to Mrs. Compton's dinner also, but he has gone aviation crazy since taking a ride at Le Bourget Field last month, and missed the dinner for an aviation lecture at the Paris School of Aviation. I wonder if he understood any of the lecture?"

"That's wonderful", said Miss Mills. "I'd love to learn to fly. I've made two air trips from London to Paris. Nothing is more thrilling. Well, I'll see you boys at the concert tonight."

"Are you singing tonight, Miss Mills?" Bill put in.

"Well, they asked me to."

"Good, then will you sing 'When a Little Blackbird Meets a Little Bluebird'?"

"Maybe I will! Au revoir."

"Well, I'll be doggone", said Braddan, "she's gone fluey, too, taking airplane rides across the English Channel. What will people do next?"

The remainder of the trip homeward was delightful. Florence Mills was encored again and again at the concerts, which Braddan and Bill never missed. The meals on board the Ile de France were wonderful also—all kinds of meats, fish, salads, desserts, and plenty of "vin rouge" (red wine).

The walks around the deck furnished good exercise, and were enjoyed by all. Reverend Braddan, however, was not so contented returning as he was going over, for Bill had given up the frequent checker and domino games with him, to sit alone on deck to think over the many fresh ideas on the proposed aviation venture that seemed to be ever crowding into his head. Braddan explained to Bill that this effervescence of ideas was due to the fact that he always drank his share of the red wine served with the meals. Of course, Bill never doubted that Braddan knew what he was talking about, for the Major always consumed his share of the wine, too.

The Statue of Liberty is always a most welcome sight to Americans returning from abroad, and, as the ship neared New York Harbor, everybody cheered the 'good old lady', as many called the statue. After disembarking at New York, Braddan and Bill had to wait till the next morning until they unloaded the Reo Flying Cloud which they had carried over with them.

En route to Chicago, Bill, who did the driving, decided to stop at the airport in each city of any size that they passed through. Yes, he might as well familiarize himself with everything aeronautical as far as possible. In New York they visited Roosevelt Field.

When they arrived in Cleveland, Bill drove immediately to the municipal airport. He parked near a swell Packard, just as a large passenger plane was coming in for a landing. As Bill got out of his car to watch the plane land, a very attractive young lady emerged from the Packard on the side nearest Bill. She watched the plane very closely, from the time it passed over the high lines until it had landed and taxied up to the hangar. Bill noticed that she was immensely interested in every movement of the plane. Her large bright eyes seemed to dance with glee when the plane made a smooth landing. The propeller blasts blew her beautiful coal black hair into her eyes. As she tossed her head to one side to shake the hair from her eyes, Bill was quite chagrined as her eyes met his staring straight at her.

"Nice landing", Bill said, trying to figure out some way of getting into conversation with her.

"Yes", she said, "I only wish I was landing that plane."

"Oh, are you a flyer?" Bill asked with joy.

"No, hope to be one some day though. I was on the field in Jacksonville, Florida, last year, when Bessie Coleman had her accident. I admired her courage to such an extent that I decided that I would become an aviatrix as soon as I got the opportunity."

"Fine. I, too, have made up my mind recently to take up aviation. I'm planning to organize a group of colored flyers to stimulate interest in aviation among members of our race. I had my first airplane ride just over a month ago in Paris, France", said Bill.

"Paris, France", she exclaimed.

"Yes, the Major and I have just returned from the American Legion Convention in Paris."

"Oh, my brother, Fred, is a Legionnaire, and contemplated going over to the convention, but couldn't get a long enough leave of absence from his work. I know he'd be tickled to meet both of you, to get first hand news of the convention. He is American Legion crazy."

"We'd be very glad to meet him, but just as soon as we get something to eat we are hitting the Dixie Highway toward Chicago. Won't you come to a restaurant with us in order that I might explain more to you about this aviation group we intend to organize?"

"Wouldn't you prefer home cooking? Brother Fred would enjoy hearing something about the convention. I can call sister Julia and have her prepare a luncheon for you, and you can tell me about the group in the meantime."

"Wonderful idea, Miss————"

"Theodore. Lottie Theodore is my name."

"Major Braddan, this is Miss Theodore; and my name is Bill Brown."

"Yes, and he has gone daffy over aviation," interrupted Braddan.

"Oh, Major, it is thrilling. Have you ever been up?"

"No, and that isn't all. I never shall go up as long as I have my right mind."

"They're selling ride tickets over there for that blue monoplane. Would you like to go up with me, Miss Theodore?" Bill asked.

"Yes, I'd love to."

"O. K.; I'll get tickets for three while you call your sister."

"For three?" exclaimed Braddan. "No, you don't. If you do you'll use two of them yourself."

They all laughed and Miss Theodore went into the 'phone booth while Bill went for the tickets.

"Give me two," said Bill, approaching the ticket seller, "for that large monoplane."

"Who are they for?" he asked.

"Er—for myself and a young lady," Bill replied, wondering why he had been asked such a question.

"Sorry sir, but we don't carry colored passengers."

"What . . ." Bill exclaimed, being taken so by surprise. He hesitated a moment, looked at the man from head to foot, but composed himself and said, "Your tickets, but my money!" and walked away, giving him a terrible look.

He then walked back to where Braddan was standing. "What's the matter, Bill?" said Braddan, who saw that something was wrong with him.

"Oh that * * * refused to sell me a ticket." Just then Miss Theodore returned. "Said they didn't carry colored passengers", Bill continued. "Miss Theodore, I didn't know such a thing was possible in Cleveland. And I haven't even taken off my American Legion cap yet. Well, that makes me all the more determined to learn aviation now. Some day I'll drop in out of the sky and tell that bird where to head in."

Soon they were trailing Miss Theodore's Packard to her sister Julia's house. On the way Bill's anger grew to a white heat, the more he thought about the refusal to carry colored passengers. What a contrast was the reception he received at this airport to the reception he received in Paris, France. His mind then drifted back to Neely and the statement he made at Le Bourget Field that day when Bill said, "There's no place like the dear old U. S. A." Neely's statement rang in his ears—"I hope you'll always feel that way."

But, on arriving at the beautiful home of Mr. and Mrs. Fred Grant at 2242 E. 81st St., Bill quite forgot the incident at the field and Neely's statement, so eager was he to tell the young lady about his plans.

Upon arrival at Cleveland, Bill had been driving over seven hours, and consequently was very hungry. But the wonderful conversation with Miss Theodore, who was so interested in aviation, made Bill quite forget his hunger until the smell of fried chicken let him know that the table was spread in the beautiful dining room.

Bill learned that the young lady had planned to make aviation her life's work, and, having just finished college, was not in a position to take up flying immediately. She had made three parachute jumps, however, in Florida, and had been taking a correspondence course in the Theory of Flight. While Rev. Braddan was telling the brother about the Paris Convention, Bill was getting the young lady's address, assuring her that he would keep in touch with her, and that she would be one of the members of the group. She assured Bill that she would join him in Chicago at the appointed time. Great progress, Bill thought. The group now had three members—Miss Theodore, Neely, and himself.

The dinner (it could not be called a luncheon) was delicious, and Bill had to remind Rev. Braddan of the day they met Florence Mills on board the Ile de France, when he admonished her for eating so much at the Compton dinner—the tables were now turned on him. After finishing that dinner, I am sure Braddan was ashamed to look a hen in the face—he had eaten so much chicken.

After taking leave of their new acquaintances, expressing their appreciation for the wonderful dinner and assuring Mrs. Grant that she was a wonderful cook, as well as assuring her that Cleveland grew a delicious brand of chicken, they headed the Flying Cloud toward Chicago.

"Quite a brilliant young lady, Bill," remarked

Braddan, as they reached the outskirts of the city, "but she, too, is flying crazy. Oh, well, I guess it's all right for those that like it. Terra firma is the place for me, and the more firmer the less terror."

They arrived in Chicago the next day, after stopping over night at the Detroit Y. M. C. A. After a few days of rest, Bill settled down to his regular business routine. All his spare time was devoted to reading aviation magazines. He subscribed for every one he ran across. His sister, who was stenographer and bookkeeper for the business, took up the role of Rev. Braddan in registering objections to his growing interest in aviation.

A couple of weeks after their arrival in Chicago, Bill received a 'phone call at his home at 7 A. M. from the garage.

"There's a man here named Neely", said the night garage man, over the 'phone to Bill.

"All right, drive him right over to the house."

In a few minutes the door bell rang, and when Bill opened the door he was greeted by a "Hello, Pal" from Neely, who was to spend three days with him before continuing his trip on to Wichita.

"I arrived rather early this morning, 6 A. M.," he said, "and figuring that was a bit too early to come by the house, I stopped at your garage and your man showed me all through. He carried me across the street to your filling station also. Say, Pal, I didn't know you had such a large business; no one would think a young fellow like you had such a business."

"Thanks for the compliment," said Bill. "Make yourself at home. You're just in time for breakfast."

"Say, Pal, no joking. You're not going to give up this business for aviation, are you?"

"If I can't sell, my sister will run the business right on. At any rate I am going into aviation for good", Bill replied.

After breakfast, Bill spent the day showing Neely

the Negro business section on the South Side, as all Chicago colored people are proud of this section and especially enjoy showing visitors about. They visited the Liberty Life Insurance Co., Bill introducing Neely to the secretary, W. Ellis Stewart, who was his classmate at the University of Illinois. Neely marvelled upon seeing nearly a hundred colored stenographers typing away, and just then the salesmen's meeting was adjourned, and over a hundred collectors, salesmen, etc., all colored, streamed out of the lecture room.

"Pal, I didn't know our people had business that large", said Neely.

"Oh, yes, and that is only one of the many places here", Bill replied.

They then visited the Chicago Defender Plant, the Binga State Bank, Overton Hygienic Manufacturing Co., Pyramid Building Loan Association, Douglass National Bank, Victory Life Insurance Co., the Chicago Whip, Provident Hospital, and other places, where hundreds of Negroes are employed by Negroes. That night they visited the Appomattox Club on South Parkway. The next day was spent in showing Neely the residential section of the South Side. They then visited the Municipal Airport, Checkerboard Field, and Heath Field.

The last day was spent going over plans for the future aviation venture, it being decided that Bill would immediately go to aviation school and learn aeronautical engineering, and that three others should be sent through school studying rigging, airplane mechanics, and flying. After this nucleus would have finished, they would be joined by Neely to carry out the project.

"You can count on me as the business manager, Pal", were Neely's last words as he boarded the train for Wichita, Kansas.

The very next day after Neely left, Bill drove to the Municipal Airport at Sixty-third and Cicero Avenue and walked into the office of the aviation school.

"Whom do you wish to see", asked the young lady at the information desk.

"I wish to see the registrar or whoever is in charge of registering new students", Bill replied.

"Just a moment, please", she said as she rang for someone.

Bill walked about looking at the many airplane pictures hanging on the wall in the office, when presently a middle aged man, very neatly dressed, appeared.

"Well?" said he, rather coldly, as he approached Bill.

"Are you the registrar?" Bill asked.

"Yes", he replied.

"My name is William Brown", Bill said, hesitating a few seconds, thinking that he would tell what his name was. However, there was no reply. "I'm interested in taking a course in aeronautics and would like to get some information in regard to your courses", Bill continued.

"Well, young man", he said, "I'm very sorry—er—but—we don't particularly cater to colored students. You see—er—it's not exactly that the policy of the school is against it, but the students themselves would walk out if there was a colored student here, and of course, since the colored students are in the minority, we have to abide by the majority in order to keep our doors open."

"How many colored students have you had?" Bill inquired.

"Oh, not any," he quickly retorted.

"Well then,———"

"But", he interrupted, "we had one to apply and I put it up to the student body, and they objected."

Bill's blood began to boil, and as dark as he was, one could see the blood coursing through his veins. His temper rose. He struggled, however, to control himself.

"I'll bet you $100 that if you allow me to address

your student body in regard to my entering the class, there will not be a single one who will object."

"Oh, yes, there will be, too, I'm sure, but you can see, my young man, that it would not be good policy to let you talk to them."

Bill didn't know what to do or say. He felt like calling him everything except a child of God, but realized that that would gain him naught. His next thought was to sock him one in the jaw, or throw the little steel model of Lindbergh's plane through the plate glass window. But the better side of him prevailed and he only gave that white gentleman a talking to he'll never forget. He emphasized that, notwithstanding the fact that he had served in the army for his country voluntarily, yet he was denied the right of paying for education he desired to get in his own country. Just then a Japanese student walked through the office, and his voice trembled as he raised his hand and said: "The day will come when you white Americans will rue the fact that you have put the Japanese, Mexican, Chinese, and in fact all foreigners, ahead of the black Americans, that you have given them all opportunities for advancement in all lines, and have denied the black American the same opportunities. Who knows", he continued, "but that some day this same Japanese might lead a squadron of Japanese bombing planes over some American city, killing, perhaps, your own mother, sister, wife, or daughter. You'd better wake up. You're cutting off your nose to spite your face. Never has it been known in history for a Negro to betray his trust to his country, yet he is always relegated to the rear, and denied things that are the very essence of his existence. Keep your old school and I'll keep my money."

With these words Bill rushed out of the office, leaving the gentleman standing motionless in the middle of the floor. Then again his mind was forced to dwell on that expression Neely made in France—"I hope you'll always feel that way."

On his way home he was so angered by his interview with the school head that he quite forgot himself, and didn't realize that he was doing sixty miles per hour down Garfield Boulevard, until a motorcycle cop drove along and motioned him to pull in to the curb. Well, he couldn't argue with the cop.

"What's the big rush?" the big Irish cop said, gruffly.

"Well, officer," said Bill, "there's no argument, I'm just wrong, that's all. My mind wasn't on what I was doing."

"Strange that you would confess that—rather unusual", retorted the cop. Then Bill related his story.

"A damn shame, Buddy. I was overseas, too. You acted pretty decent though, about it. 'Spec I would o' tore up the joint", he continued. "Guess I won't give you a ticket this time, but get your mind on your driving now, and don't let another cop catch you speeding like that, 'cause he may not be a veteran."

"Well", Bill said to himself, "there are some good white folks, too."

On his way home he drove over to Rev. Braddan's home at 58th and Wabash Avenue. Depressed, Bill related his experience to the Reverend. He was really upset. It took a great deal to upset Bill, but his limit was just about reached this time, because he thought that if a colored man could not get what he wanted in Chicago, then it just couldn't be had here in this country.

"Reverend Braddan", said Bill, "I feel like going back there with a shotgun and blowing every official out of the school."

"Calm yourself, Bill", interrupted Braddan. "It is true that intelligent and self-respecting Negroes cannot accept the precept of our American democracy and respect its constitution and honor its flag, if they must be subjected to social degradation, industrial oppression, legal injustice, and be politically outlawed and oppressed. Yet survive they must, both politically and economically. Who but our prophets and redeemers shall teach them that not through the doors of Socialism or Communism lies their escape, but that the key to deliverance and the sceptre of power lie in the strength of their own minds and spirits. When they honor their own personality and believe in themselves with all the exalted fervor with which a saint believes in his God, sacrifice, martyrdom, and loss shall be willing tributes to pay the final triumphs of a people whose spirit is victorious against every weapon that may be formed against it."

"Wonderful philosophy", Bill thought. And so it was, that whenever he was depressed he always went to Rev. Braddan, and was soon relieved by his wonderful counsel.

He was quite restless that night. While lying in bed wondering which way to turn next, he thought about enlisting in the Army Air Corps. So next day bright and early he hit the road for Rantool, Illinois. There, the army air school is located just six miles from Urbana, where Bill attended the University of Illinois.

Arriving at headquarters, Bill was greeted by a very pleasant lieutenant, who asked him what he could do for him. Bill replied that he wanted to learn aviation and wished to enlist in the Army Air Corps.

"Well, young man, the air service is the branch to get into all right, but we don't take enlistments unless they've completed at least two years of college work successfully."

"Then I guess I'm just in line. I graduated from the University of Illinois", said Bill enthusiastically.

"So", the lieutenant said, calmly. "Fine. And another requirement is that the applicants must be students in engineering. You see, in order to understand navigation, rigging, aerodynamics, etc., and many of the formulas in aeronautical engineering, one must have an appreciable knowledge of mathematics and geometry, hence we specify engineering students."

"Today certainly must be my lucky day", Bill yelled. "I graduated in electrical engineering, and ask me if that course isn't full of mathematics; why I've had mathematics through the theory of equations, multiple integrals, integration of rational fractions—and don't talk about geometry — descriptive geometry, spherical geometry—all of them. I don't believe there could be any more."

"Oh, is that so?" replied the lieutenant, slowly. "Then I guess you win. Suppose I'll have to confess now. You see, it's just like this. I thought I might be able to save you a little embarrassment had I found out that you were not a college man and so well fortified, but to be frank, and you might as well know it, it is the policy of the War Department not to accept colored men in the air corps. Personally, I think it is a darn shame. But what can I do? You're not the first colored lad that has been here, but I got rid of the first two quite easily, because neither had been to college, and the last one who was a college graduate had no engineering—he studied agriculture at the university. I, personally, don't agree with such a policy. I was born in South Carolina, and was reared by a colored mammy, and would just as soon instruct colored students as whites. In fact, the colored fellows are much easier to get along with. But—such is life! Why don't you go to a commercial school of aviation? Haven't you got the money?"

"Yes, I have the money, but I've been turned down just like I have been here, only not as courteously."

The lieutenant laughed, and said, "Thanks for the compliment. Do you live near here? During spare times I'd be very glad to give you private lessons."

"I'm afraid I live too far. Chicago is 120 miles

from here. Anyway, I wanted to put all my time to it, and get it from the ground up and get through with it. I wanted to learn aeronautical engineering, flying, and mechanics also."

"That's different. I only teach flying. How many schools did you try?"

"Only one here in the United States, so far. On the other hand, I have a standing invitation to enter the Paris School of Aviation any time, but I'd rather study here."

"Too bad, and I hate to turn down an intelligent fellow like you, but any time you are down this way, I'll be glad to give you flying instructions."

After thanking him for his offer, Bill headed the Reo back toward Chicago, but remembered this time not to speed, because the cops on the road to Kankakee were really on the job. Same old thing, Bill thought, but this time it was Uncle Sam himself.

The first thing Bill did upon returning to the office was to dictate a letter to Neely in Wichita, explaining what he was going through. A few days later the following letter was received from Neely:

"Dear Bill:
    Hope you'll always feel that way.
    Keep trying.
                                    Burrell Neely."

This letter angered Bill so much that before he cooled off he had posted a letter to Neely asking him why in h—— he didn't make a suggestion as to what to do. A night letter the next day from Neely begged Bill's pardon, but stated that he had made a suggestion, which was—keep trying.

In about three days, Bill received a copy of the Negro Star from Wichita. This edition of the Star had nearly a half of the front page devoted to the return of Burrell Neely from the convention in Paris, with his picture very prominently displayed on the front page, thus showing that he was a big shot in his town.

Two months had elapsed. Bill had written to several schools that were advertised in magazines—Peoria, New York, Cincinnati, Kansas City—explaining to each that he was colored. In each case he received similar replies—nothing doing.

One day he met an old college chum from St. Louis, named Victor LaNier Hicks, who told him of a large aviation school in St. Louis that he was sure would take colored students, because they had written him. Somewhat brightened by this new prospect, Bill drove to St. Louis Saturday morning, in order to spend Sunday afternoon visiting a school teacher friend whom he admired greatly, Miss Josephine Harris.

Monday morning early he went to the airport, and if ever he came near losing his good Baptist religion it was at this time, for, till this day, he has not been able to see the vice president who was supposed to be in charge of admitting new students, notwithstanding the fact that he remained in St. Louis five days.

By this time he was quite depressed, although more determined than ever to learn aeronautics. "Looks as though I'll have to go to France after all", he said, perusing a new flying magazine he had just purchased, "Western Flying." "Quite an interesting magazine", he observed. There seemed to be more flying activity out West than anywhere else. "What's this?" A very attractive advertisement caught his eye. "Students are coming from all parts of the country to the Warren College of Aeronautics in Los Angeles where the sun shines the year round."

"Well, it won't hurt. I believe I'll write just one more school before I definitely decide to go to Paris to study aeronautics", said Bill to himself. And so he did, stating that he was colored and giving his qualifications, etc.

Three weeks later, to his great surprise, when he

had given up all hope, a letter from C. A. Warren, president, stated that they had three Japanese students, one Chinaman, two Filipinos, one Mexican, one Hindu, and over a hundred whites, and that he saw no reason why he should not have a colored student.

"Hooray, I'm off for Los Angeles", yelled Bill after reading the letter, and the whole community soon learned about it.

CHAPTER III

A wire to Neely immediately followed, signifying his intention of stopping off in Wichita en route to Los Angeles. A further communication with the Warren School informed Bill that his course in aeronautical engineering and flying would cost $1,000. This did not include room and board. The time required was estimated at one year, providing Bill could attend the day and night sessions. Bill then wrote the president of the school that he had two men who were very good automobile mechanics whom he wished to put through aviation engine mechanics and airplane mechanics. Return mail informed Bill that they would be accepted, each course to run $350.

The entire South Side soon knew that Bill, Rogers, and Wooten were to motor to Los Angeles to study aeronautics. The Chicago Defender, Chicago Whip, and Chicago Bee printed several columns about it, carrying Bill's picture.

The following week Bill received a letter which read as follows:

"Dear Mr. Brown:

I note with pleasure, although with great surprise, in the Chicago Defender, that you are leaving soon for Los Angeles to enter the aviation school. I wondered why you went so far, although I realize that there is good flying weather there the year round. I was trying to make arrangements to come to Chicago to join the group at the proper time, but now it looks as though I must go to Los Angeles, which seems almost impossible for me. However, I shall not give up hope. I hope to be able to join the group in Los Angeles some day. I tried to get in school here, but was refused. Wishing you much success, I remain

Yours for the advancement of Negro aviation,

LOTTIE THEODORE."

This letter made Bill very blue. It is one of the things that made him more determined, for he realized that there were thousands of other boys and girls throughout America craving an opportunity to learn aeronautics. While pondering over this letter, Bill was called to answer the 'phone.

"Hello, Mr. Brown, this is Mrs. Helen White."

"Oh, how do you do, Mrs. White, I haven't heard your lovely voice for quite some time. How are you?"

"Just fine, thanks. Say, Mr. Brown, there is a young man here from New York who says he's an aviator. Knowing you were leaving soon to take up aviation, I thought you'd like to meet him."

"Yes, I would. Thank you so much, Mrs. White. I'll be right up."

In a few minutes Bill drove up in front of the Overton Building, and went upstairs to the office of the Chicago Bee, colored newspaper, from whence came the 'phone call. Upon entering the office, he was attracted by the sound of a loud but very cultured voice. Glancing in the direction of the voice, Bill noticed a tall, handsomely dressed young man, who had passed behind the swinging gates which separate the customers from the office employees, and, in a loud voice, this highly perfumed gentleman was telling all of the fifty or more stenographers and bookkeepers in the office that he was the only Negro aviator in America and had come to Chicago to make a parachute jump on Decoration Day over the grave of Bessie Coleman.

Seeing Bill enter the office, Mrs. White, who was the head office girl, spoke up saying, "Oh, here is Mr. Brown", whereupon, this young man who had seemingly assumed command of the entire office strode in Bill's direction with his right hand extended—

"Come right on back, Mr. Brown", he said, "I'm Lieut. Hubert Julian, from New York. I'm sure you have read about me. I'm the one who attempted a transatlantic flight in 1919, long before the idea ever struck Lindbergh. I had a little motor trouble, unfortunately, and I was forced down in Flushing Bay, just barely escaping with my life. I have made parachute jumps right into the heart of New York. I am the foremost parachute jumper in the world. I understand you are planning to take up aviation."

"Yes, yes", Bill interrupted with much difficulty. "I'm certainly glad to meet you."

Then Julian kissed Mrs. White's hand very gracefully as did the knights of old—bowed graciously to all the young ladies in the office, assuring each of them that he would see her in the near future, took Bill by the arm, and they both left the office, leaving the girls in an uproar of glee.

Learning that the newcomer had just arrived in town and had not as yet selected a hotel, Bill invited him to stay with him, which invitation he very readily accepted, explaining that Bill had been so highly recommended to him, and that he always tried to get into an aeronautical environment wherever he went. Bill carried his suitcases and put them in the car and soon they were speeding down Michigan Boulevard toward home.

After chatting a bit about the beautiful Chicago boulevards, homes, etc., they arrived at Bill's home. As soon as the lieutenant had washed and changed clothes, he showed Bill his wardrobe, which consisted of all silk shirts, silk pajamas, silk underwear, silk gloves, silk socks, and two very expensive suits besides the one he wore.

"Now, come sit here, Mr. Brown, and tell me your plans," he then said, very dignified. This was said in a

very commanding manner, and ordinarily Bill would
have done everything else but accede to the will of one
so commanding in his speech, but there was something
peculiar about this fellow, and so Bill obeyed.

"Well, you see, I have recently been awakened to
the wonderful opportunities in aviation, and, seeing a
great opportunity and opening for employment for
numbers of my race, I decided to learn aviation to help
stimulate interest in the industry among Negroes, by
giving educational demonstrations, exhibitions, and
lectures."

"Brown, you have at last struck the keynote. I
admire your pluck. It's just what the young Negro
should do, get into a field of industry. The day has
come when our young men must think of something
else besides law and medicine. We must become producers, and aviation is as good a field as any to start
in. I congratulate myself on being the first. Congratulations to you on being the second. I started in 1918.
I'm ten years ahead of you."

With difficulty Bill broke in. "Er—I thought Bessie
Coleman was first."

"Oh, no," he replied sharply. "She was after me.
Pardon, I erred. You're third. But, getting down to
the point," he continued, in English that was as good
as any Bill had ever heard, "when and where do you
intend to start your aeronautical training?"

"I have just about made up my mind to go to Los
Angeles to enter the Warren School of Aeronautics,
after having been turned down here and in several
other places because I was colored."

"Oh, I could have told you that at first. You see, I
got mine in Canada, in the Canadian Air Force. Let's
see," said he, pausing a moment and touching his forehead as though in great contemplation—"No, no, you
won't go to Los Angeles—you'll come with me. I'll
teach you. You have a good car in which we could
travel from place to place and give lectures and raise

funds for our transatlantic flight that we will make in
the fall, and you will be my co-pilot."

"Co-pilot?" Bill exclaimed. "Man, I know nothing
at all about flying, and I never attempt anything unless
I know what I am doing."

"Oh, tut, tut", he replied, "I'll teach you everything
necessary for you to know. With that finished, now
let's talk about what I came here for. I'm sure you
know Rev. J. C. Austin, Pastor of the Pilgrim Baptist
Church?"

"Yes", said Bill.

"He's a wonderful man, and quite interested in the
Negroes' progress in aviation. In 1919 he raised $500
and then added $500 himself, thus making up the first
thousand dollars paid on the plane I attempted to fly
across the Atlantic. After I crashed in Flushing Bay,
I thought he was through, but evidently not, for I com-
municated with him in regard to my making a parachute jump over the grave of Bessie Coleman, Decoration Day, and his church is going to sponsor the jump,
and also a monument to be unveiled to Bessie on that
day, after I jump."

"Gee, that will be swell", Bill interrupted.

"And you will ride over in the ship with me when
I jump."

This last statement was the first thing the visitor
said that interested Bill.

"Fine," he said, "I'll enjoy it immensely."

Soon after lunch Julian took the 'phone book, found
the address of a parachute dealer, and asked Bill to
drive him there. When they left the place they had
purchased a second-hand parachute for $150. Julian
then instructed Bill to drive him to the residence of
Rev. Austin.

Before leaving the pastor's house, Julian had succeeded in getting the pastor to give him a check for
$150 for the parachute.

That night he dictated a letter, signed it, and handed it to Bill.

Julian Airplane Fund
TRANS-ATLANTIC FLIGHT

SENATOR A SPENCER FELD
CHAIRMAN
12 EAST 41ST STREET
NEW YORK CITY

CAPTAIN T. M. DENT
EXECUTIVE SECRETARY
WHITTIER 0425

BEULAH A. YOUNG
DETROIT PEOPLES NEWS
TREASURER

DETROIT BRANCH

4326 MILFORD AVE

WALNUT 1108

Detroit, Mich.
May 23, 1928.

Lieut. Wm. J. Powell,
4627 S Wabash Ave.,
Chicago, Ill.

Dear Lieut:

It is a pleasure for me to inform you that after due and careful consideration, I have this day decided to appoint you co-pilot and chief mechanic on my trans-Alantic flight to Rome and return.

From the references submitted, I have every reason to believe that you are the type of man desired for so hazardous an undertaking.

Assuring you that I will do every thing in my power to make our flight a safe and successful on for the good and benefit of our Race, and bring to them that immortal glory of Aeronautical fame.

Hoping that you will prepare yourself physically and mentally for the strain that such a flight necessitate, I have the pleasure to be

Yours for the Race Advancement,

....
Lieut. Hubert Julian.

The next morning they drove to the parachute dealer's, and returned with the parachute to the church where, with the assistance of Rev. Austin and the janitor, the parachute was suspended from the top of the church, hanging over the pulpit in the main auditorium. This was the closest Bill had ever been to a parachute, and he marvelled at its enormous size. It stretched from the ceiling almost to the floor.

The next day was Sunday. The church was packed, as usual—about 3,000 people. Rev. Austin, one of the best speakers in the ministry, preached a wonderful sermon, but did not hold the attention of the audience, for that big silk bag hanging there was a mystery to everyone. Finishing his remarks, Rev. Austin told the audience that he didn't want a single person to leave, for he wanted to present a very distinguished person who had a message for them, and who would explain what that contraption was hanging there for. The choir sang only as a Negro choir can sing, while a large collection was raised for the church.

Then he introduced Lieut. Hubert Julian as the only Negro aviator in the world. There was great applause. All the while Julian was bowing gracefully, as only he could bow. Presently the applause ceased and Julian began an eloquent discourse which bordered from time to time upon a lecture, an oration, and a sermon. He flayed the race for always bringing up the rear in everything—he deplored the fact that Bessie Coleman had passed and left him—the only Negro aviator in such a large field—but stated that he would pioneer the trail provided he could get the cooperation of his people. Really he was a wonderful speaker. His eloquence almost equalled that of Rev. Austin. If someone could rid Julian of his spasmodic outbursts of egotism there could hardly be a speaker found to excel him.

He wound up his speech with an impassioned plea for funds to purchase the parachute hanging in the church and for a monument to Bessie Coleman, over whose grave he would jump Decoration Day, about ten days hence. At the direction of Rev. Austin the choir again sang and the audience, almost to a man, rose and marched up to the table with contributions. Then the baskets were passed. While other visitors were introduced, the money was counted. Then the lieutenant rose to thank the congregation for the $813 which had been received. He then asked them to bring up another dollar, stating that he wasn't superstitious but didn't like the number 13. Five more dollars were brought up.

Decoration Day came. Thousands of people crowded into the cemetery to see the parachute jump. The monument was in place with a veil around it. On each side of the monument was a little basket into which dimes, nickels, quarters, and even dollars were being dropped to defray the cost of the parachute and the monument.

After driving him to the Municipal Airport, Bill's sister took the car and drove on to the cemetery, leaving Bill and Julian at the airport with the parachute. Near the appointed time Julian endeavored to strap the parachute on, but he didn't seem to be able to get the straps just right. Of course it was all Greek to Bill. "Oh, I'll straighten it out all right," said Julian. "I know all about 'chutes. I've been packing them for quite some time."

But he couldn't get it straightened out, or else didn't want to. The time grew late. It was past the appointed hour. Soon came a 'phone call from Rev. Austin at the cemetery. Julian sent Bill over to answer the 'phone and to tell the Reverend they'd be over the cemtery shortly. He unpacked the 'chute partly. Soon an army officer came over and offered to straighten it out for him, but Julian refused to allow anyone to touch it. Time went on. A couple more 'phone calls with the same reply, Bill refusing, however, to answer the 'phone again. Presently Bill heaved a sigh of relief as Julian pronounced the parachute O. K. at last. He then told Bill to watch the parachute very closely while he went over to inform the pilot who was to fly him that he was ready.

Soon, he returned. "Isn't that hell, Bill?" he said rather nonchalantly. "What are we going to do?"

"What's the matter?" asked Bill.

"The pilot said I waited too long, and now he has a long trip to make."

"Can't you get another plane?" Bill said, frantically.

"Not another fellow on the field will carry me", was his reply.

Bill was disgusted, and furthermore, how would they get away? Bill's car was at the cemetery. While they bemoaned their terrible plight, with thousands of people anxiously awaiting the much heralded parachute jump at the cemetery, a good natured fellow stepped up and said he'd drive them over to the cemetery in the air corps truck of which he was the driver. So the three piled up on the front seat which was high and open, Julian hanging the parachute over his back, a comical sight. Arriving at the cemetery in an army truck! The Chicago Defender reporters were certainly on the job, for the paper came out with a headline that "Lieut. Julian flew in an army truck."

This affair caused a great setback to Negro aviation, for a great champion of Negro progress, Rev. Austin, was disappointed.

Several days later, Julian, quite perturbed over the fact that Bill would not accompany him East on a lecture tour, left for Detroit, but not until he had enticed Bill to let him have a Chevrolet sedan that was for sale in Bill's garage. He stated that the money would be sent back for it just as soon as he arrived in Detroit. But Bill never heard from him again until three years later.

On the 15th day of June, 1928, the Reo Flying Cloud was packed and made ready for the trip westward to Los Angeles, when Rev. Braddan drove up in front of Bill's place.

"Well, Bill, I drove by to wish you good luck", the chaplain said, getting out of his car.

"Thank you, Reverend. Good luck from you is worth a million good lucks, especially on an aviation project."

Braddan laughed. "So you are going to train up a group of Negroes to pioneer aviation in the race?"

"That's it," Bill said cheerfully. "A group of ten trained in all the major branches of aeronautics—one engine mechanic, one airplane mechanic, one navigator, one parachute rigger, one aeronautical engineer, one radio man, one parachute jumper, and three good flyers."

"And when do you expect to return?"

"As soon as we finish training. Then we will tour the country. Chicago, of course, will be one of the first stops, in an endeavor to stimulate a real organized and comprehensive effort to develop aeronautics among Negroes."

"Then I'll make you a bargain, Bill," said Braddan, seeming to be getting very serious. "You know I never intend to take a ride in an airplane."

"Yes, so you've said before," said Bill puzzled.

"But if you can get a group of ten Negroes together to pioneer a new field, and if you can keep them intact long enough to complete their training, and then get them all to Chicago, then I'll take a ride with you."

"That's a bargain", said Bill, and they shook hands before Bill had time to consider just what Braddan was driving at.

"Good luck, Bill. Write often and return soon."

Bill reflected awhile as Braddan drove away. He could always depend on wise counsel from Braddan, but what prompted him to make this statement? "He

certainly must not have much confidence in the race
sticking together," thought Bill, "or he's just saying
that to put me on my guard. He has his own way of
doing that."

And so the next day, Bill, Rogers, and Wooten were
westward bound.

Their first stop of any duration was at Wichita,
as the guests of Mr. and Mrs. Burrell Neely. They
stayed with Neely five days, perfecting plans for
the future venture, and visiting the many airports in
Wichita. On one occasion Neely introduced Bill to Mr.
Walter Beech in the office of the Travellaire, where the
three had an extended talk on aviation. Mr. Beech,
who was then president of the Travellaire, thought the
plan a wonderful one, and pledged his support.

After being most royally entertained and reducing
the number of poultry in the State of Kansas considerably, they departed for Los Angeles.

On the second day of August, just about one year
from the time that Neely and Bill decided to take up
aeronautics, they crossed the Los Angeles County line.

CHAPTER IV

BILL LEARNS TO FLY

Los Angeles, the metropolis of California, with its bright sunshine, was to be Bill's school campus for a year and a half. The first thing he did was to rent a beautiful Spanish type bungalow, completely furnished, on West 29th Street. He lost no time in enrolling at the Warren College of Aeronautics, which was then located on Slauson Avenue. He decided to taboo parties, wiener bakes, whist tournaments, etc., and put in all his time studying aeronautics. One of his fraternity brothers (Alpha Phi Alpha), Walter Gordon, having heard of Bill's fraternal activities at the University of Illinois, induced him to pull just one party by way of an introduction to the social set of the Angel City. But aside from that, everything was aerodynamics, wing curves, streamline forms, rhumb line, and other familiar aeronautical terms.

At Warren School, Bill became a favorite, for in the engineering room he excelled. He was very good in mathematics, and of course, the difficult formulas were, as he put it, "right down his alley." The president of the school, Mr. Warren, found time to enter ofttimes into council with Bill, especially after he learned of Bill's plans.

"Yes", he said one day to Bill, as the two sat talking in the president's office, "it's the only way, Bill; you must first prepare yourself. Then, with a good aeronautical foundation, any young colored man at this time has a wonderful opportunity. But the great trouble with many of your race is that they step out into things without being fully prepared. There's a young colored lad here in town who had a splendid chance. They call him 'Ace' Foreman. He certainly had a lot of nerve. He got an old Jenny fuselage, opened up a school on Central Avenue, and enrolled over 200 colored students in a club, at $10 a member.

"They actually covered the fuselage, built the wings, put in an old motor, and pronounced the ship ready to fly, without even calling in a Department of Commerce inspector for an inspection. I don't think he even knew it was necessary to have an inspection. He had never been to a school of aeronautics, but just picked up what he knew from reading books and hanging around the airports. I tried to get him to enter school here one day when he came over to buy an OX5 piston, for I knew with the proper training he would have been a wizard, but he felt as though he knew enough. Bill, he carried that ship out to the field, and it actually flew up about 75 feet before it cracked up, injuring himself and another boy named Al Barrett. But the ship flew and the colored people were elated.

"So 'Ace' bought another Jenny that was not fit to fly across the street, and wasn't licensed, and he and another fellow by the name of Artis Ward announced their intentions of making the first Negro transcontinental flight. Led by a Mr. J. B. Bass, editor of a colored weekly paper called the California Eagle, and Dr. Hudson of the N.A.A.C.P., I am told, the colored people contributed several hundred dollars for this flight. One of the boys told me that they took off amid the cheers of several thousand people, then flew to Salt Lake City where they wired back for more funds, which were sent them immediately. It is said they then flew to Chicago, hauled the plane through the streets of Chicago, and placed it in storage, stating that the plane was not in condition to go farther. 'Ace' always wore an immaculate uniform with boots and a Sam Browne belt. I don't hear much of him lately since the government fined him $500 for violation of the Air Commerce Act. They will probably send him to prison for that. Too bad; that fellow had a wonderful brain. So, Bill, get your training first. And the more you get, the better off you'll be, and never violate any of the rules of the Air Commerce Act of 1926."

Aeronautical engineering was quite interesting to Bill. He especially liked navigation and meteorology, having made his highest grades in these studies and "aircraft design." But when the flight instructor at the Warren School, Mr. A. E. Monteith, told him to get ready to go to take a physical examination in preparation to start flying, he was thrilled beyond words. He could hardly wait until the day came for his first lesson.

"Here's a copy of the Air Commerce Rules and Regulations; learn the Air Traffic Laws and when you know them thoroughly, let me know," said Mr. Monteith to Bill.

A week later Bill went to his instructor and notified him that he had learned the Air Traffic Laws. "Are you sure?" asked Mr. Monteith, "then we'll see ..."

Q. "What is the penalty for violation of the air traffic laws?"

Ans. "A civil penalty of $500."

Q. "Do the rules apply to unlicensed pilots?"

Ans. "Yes. They apply to all pilots."

Q. "What distance is required between airplanes in flight?"

Ans. "300 feet."

Q. "What is the minimum altitude in flying over cities or towns?"

Ans. "Sufficient altitude must be maintained to permit of a reasonably safe emergency landing, but in no case less than 1,000 feet."

Q. "What is the minimum altitude while flying over open country?"

Ans. "500 feet."

Q. "May acrobatics be performed with pay passengers?"

Ans. "No."

Q. "What's the rule regarding intoxicating liquors and drugs?"

Ans. "Pilots' licenses may be suspended or revoked for being under the influence of liquors or drugs while flying or for carrying passengers who are obviously under the influence of the same."

Q. "When must lights be displayed on airplanes?"

Ans. "At all times during flight between one-half hour after sunset and one-half hour before sunrise."

Q. "Is it permissible to do acrobatics over a city or town?"

Ans. "No."

"Well young fellow," said Mr. Monteith, "that's pretty good. I guess you are about ready to take your examination for your student pilot's permit. You are supposed to know the Air Traffic Laws."

"Oh, do they give you an examination on Air Traffic Laws to get the student pilots' permit?" Bill inquired.

"No, they only give you a physical examination, but you must state that you know the Air Traffic Laws thoroughly."

And so the next day Bill went to the Medical Building on Wilshire Boulevard, to the office of Lyster and Jones. After telling the young lady that he was sent there by Mr. Monteith for his physical examination, she brought out the applications for student pilot's permit, and Bill filled them out and signed them. The fee was ten dollars, with fifty cents notary charge. He was then ushered into the examination room. Sight of the doctor caused his heart to beat faster, and the first thing the doctor did was to examine his heart. Then his eyes, lungs, ears, nose were examined. After a strenuous examination, hopping around on one foot, calling off letters in the eye test, telling what had been spoken to him in whispers, distinguishing between colors, straight lines, circles, curves, etc., Bill was finally pronounced O. K. With a sigh of relief he was shown the way back to the girl's desk, where he was given his student pilot's permit.

This permit authorized him to receive flying instructions and to operate a plane only in the vicinity of the field from which he received instructions.

The day for the first lesson arrived. Bill was at Lincoln Airport half an hour earlier than the appointed time, watching the planes take off and land. Presently Mr. Monteith arrived. He instructed the mechanic to get the plane warmed up. He then began to lecture to Bill.

"Now, Bill—you are going to sit in the pilot's cockpit" (rear seat) "and I'll be in the front cockpit. You have already learned that the plane has dual controls" (the plane used was a Waco nine) "which means that you can fly the ship, or I can fly it from the front. But, to start with, I am going to take the plane off the ground up to an altitude of 2,000 feet or more, and don't you touch the controls until I tell you through the gossport" (speaking tube). "After we get sufficient altitude, I will tell you to take the plane, or rather, to take the stick only. You are to try to keep the nose of the ship 'on the horizon', in other words, keep the nose level. Don't let it go up or down. In your theory of flight, what kind of 'stability' would you call that?"

"That would be longitudinal stability, or equilibrium about the lateral axis."

"Yes, and how would you maintain this longitudinal stability?"

"The horizontal tail surfaces control motion about the lateral axis. By pushing the stick forward the ship noses down. By pulling back on the stick the nose comes up."

"O. K., but don't be too heavy on the stick—pull it back and push it forward gently. Not suddenly. And then, after you can keep the nose on the horizon, I'll give you over the lateral control of the plane—lateral stability, as you know, is equilibrium about the horizontal axis, that is, keeping the wings level. In order to do that you push the stick over in the direction of the high wing. If you notice your left wing low, push the stick over to the right. If the left wing is high, push the stick to the left. Don't bother about the rudder. I'll handle that until you learn to handle the stick."

And so they both climbed into the plane; shortly the plane was up in the air. Bill had on a helmet containing two holes into which the speaking tubes conveyed Monteith's messages to his ears. At 2,000 feet altitude, the piercing voice of Mr. Monteith came through the gossport.

"All right, Bill—take the stick. Keep the nose on the horizon."

So Bill took the stick for the first time. What a thrill, he was himself helping to fly the ship! But hardly did he get the stick into his hands when the nose of the ship shot up as though it had hit a bump or gust or something; but Bill calmly pushed forward on the stick too much, for the nose dropped 'way below the horizon; then he pulled back on it, overdoing it each time. And so this process kept up until the instructor grabbed the stick and steadied it with the nose on the horizon.

"You're too heavy on the stick, just take it easy", said Monteith through the tube.

From time to time, however, the nose would keep bobbing either up or down, which kept Bill very busy keeping it on the horizon. Ten minutes of this with the instructor correcting him at intervals, then he was told to keep the lateral balance also. This added much to Bill's already occupied mind. And it was no easy job for him now. He had to watch the nose and horizon, and both wings.

"Get that left wing up", yelled Mr. Monteith, and slowly Bill pushed the stick to the right, looking from one wing to the other, only to be yelled at again— "Nose down." And so this kept up for half an hour, which seemed like half a day to Bill. He longed to get back to the ground. His hand was tired from gripping the stick, and to make it worse, the goggles he had purchased didn't fit his nose, and every time he looked out from behind the windshield, the wind rushing under the goggles brought tears to his eyes, until now he could not see at all. Mr. Monteith was yelling, "Nose up, nose down, right wing low, left wing high", etc., but it was of no use. Bill couldn't see a thing. Tears had flooded his eyes and the wind had blown them all over the lenses in the goggles. Good thing the half hour was up, for he was helpless. Once back on the ground he drew a sigh of relief.

"Well, how'd you like it? Do you think you'll ever make a flyer?" asked the instructor.

Bill only laughed. He was wiping his eyes and drying the lenses in his goggles. He then immediately drove to Nicholas Beasely's airplane store and purchased a pair of goggles that fitted his face. He slept but little that night. He "held the joy-stick" all night long in his dreams.

The next day he was at the field early, as usual, but Mr. Monteith didn't show up. After waiting an hour and a half, Bill went to a 'phone and called him, telling him that he had been waiting at the field two hours.

"What kind of an aviator do you call yourself?" asked Mr. Monteith over the 'phone. "Don't you see that the ceiling is just about 500 feet? You can't fly with those clouds hanging that low." But Bill had not noticed that. His mind was absorbed in how to keep those wings level and the nose on the horizon.

Four days elapsed before the clouds and fog permitted student flying. But Bill went to the field every day just the same. The fifth day was bright and clear.

Bill was on hand bright and early as usual, but the mechanic could not get the plane started. They drained the carburetor jets, tested the magneto spark, cranked, and cranked, and cranked, but to no avail. Finally the mechanic announced there would be no flying, that he was going to check the valve clearances and spark plug gaps.

Nearly a week had gone by, and only one flying lesson of a half an hour! Anxious as Bill was to get his lessons, this was most disgusting. Next day, however, the ship was ready, and he went up for his second lesson. Ten minutes in the air, and he had no trouble at all keeping the nose and wings in the proper place. It seemed to have come to him during this period of waiting and having a chance to think it out. So Mr. Monteith landed the plane.

"Now, Bill, I'm going to let you use the rudder in conjunction with the stick. The rudder is the means of getting 'directional stability', that is, control about the vertical axis. If you wish to turn left, you 'give 'er left rudder', that is, push with the left foot. But the main thing to remember about turning is that you never turn without banking at the same time. Banking is to incline the ship over in the direction in which you wish to turn. If you use the left rudder, then give it left stick also, or right stick with right rudder. This is done to keep the plane from 'skidding' or 'slipping.' Do you notice that when a boy turns a corner on a bicycle he leans the bicycle in the direction in which he wishes to turn? That is the same principle here, and the correct amount to bank a ship can only be learned through practice. In a left turn, if the air rushes against your right cheek, then you are giving too much rudder. And vice versa in a right turn. All right, let's go. I'll give you all the controls at 2,000 feet."

And soon the plane was in the air again. At 2,000 feet Bill was given over all the controls.

"Follow that highway", said the instructor, pointing down to a highway running straight north and south. So Bill looked over the side of the ship and proceeded to follow the highway. This he did very well, except he just couldn't keep that left wing up. It seemed to stay low all the time.

"Now make a 180 degree turn to the left and follow the same highway."

So Bill pushed the left rudder and banked the ship to the left, but banking to the left scared him. He felt as though he was tipping over too far and was going to fall out, so he snatched the stick back to the right, but his left foot still pressed the rudder, causing the ship to skid terribly in the turn, and the wind rushed into the ship as if a hurricane was coming. The instructor grabbed the controls and yelled to Bill to follow him through. He then executed a perfect left turn, then a right turn, and then instructed Bill to try it.

Bill did much better this time. He soon was able to bank the ship over and not feel as though he was falling out. The time passed much faster today. After several turns, the instructor told him to head back to the airport, but he might as well have said to the Rock of Gibraltar, for Bill had no idea where he was. The instructor then took the controls, and in less than one minute had closed the throttle for a glide to the airport, which was just off to the left a little. Thus ended the second lesson.

The next day Bill was again given turns to the right and left, 180 degree turns, then advanced to 360 degree turns. His turns were good, but he just couldn't keep that left wing up—strange—as soon as he took his mind directly off that left wing, it would drop, as Bill said.

The fourth lesson was also devoted to turns and that left wing, as were the fifth and sixth lessons. Three hours on his log book! Bill now felt very proud.

It wouldn't be long at this rate until he would solo, he thought.

The seventh lesson he was shown how to use the throttle in the air.

"We're cruising at 1380 R.P.M., so watch your tachometer, and adjust the throttle accordingly", cautioned the instructor. "If for any reason the motor stops or revs down below 1380, push the stick forward and keep the ship in a glide. Why should you do that?" he asked.

"If the motor stops, nosing the ship downward will cause the plane to maintain flying speed, otherwise it would stall and spin," Bill replied.

"O.K. Let's go. I'll give it to you at 2,000 feet."

And so at 2,000 feet, the controls were turned over to Bill. Hardly had this been done when the throttle closed. Not knowing just exactly what had caused the motor to slow down, Bill started looking everywhere, bewildered. Just then Mr. Monteith yelled, "Get that nose down! What do you want to do, stall the ship?" And immediately he took over the controls himself, dived the plane sufficiently to pick up speed, and then let Bill take it again.

Well, well, how quickly one can forget, thought Bill. He had been cautioned about flying speed of the plane just before they went up, and yet was taken off his feet by surprise when the throttle was closed. But the next time he was "on" to it. Mr. Monteith tried this stunt three or four times, before he brought the ship to the ground. Bill was getting used to the air now. He could even find his way back to the airport. He had had seven hours in the air. He was making nice figure eights. But when was he to start take-offs and landings? He had read about most of the fellows in the army soloing in five or six hours. He was getting uneasy. So, today he said to the instructor: "I guess I must be pretty dumb. I've had seven hours flying and haven't soloed yet. Some fellows solo in five hours and I'm not even on take-offs and landings yet."

"Well, I won't exactly say that you're not so dumb, but I will say that Monteith will never solo anyone in five hours, or seven either. That is the reason there are so many accidents. Before I solo anyone he must go through side slips, spins, stalls, recovering from stalls, figure eights, and vertical banks as well. A man can't do that in five hours and make decent landings too. So let's get going, I'll give it to you at 2,000 feet."

At 2,000 feet Bill again took over the controls, starting his eighth hour of instruction. After executing some fairly decent figure eights, he was instructed to climb to 5,000 feet. He had never been to this height before, but he pulled up the nose into a steep climb, only to be yelled at by Mr. Monteith to climb gradually, and the customary, "Do you want to stall the ship?" What a feeling—5,000 feet up! It seemed that the higher he went the more secure he felt. At 5,000 feet, Mr. Monteith took over the controls. He closed the throttle and pulled the stick back.

"Watch it stall", he said to Bill, and the plane slowed up, the controls became sloppy, and the nose of the ship started to fall off to the left just as Mr. Monteith pushed the stick 'way forward, and the plane gained speed and recovered from the stall. He then turned the controls over to Bill, instructing him to practice it, which he did very successfully, twice; but the third time Bill got the scare of his lifetime. He pulled the stick back and the plane slowed up, the controls got sloppy as usual, but before he nosed the ship downward, the nose fell off to the left itself, and then such a sensation as Bill had never before experienced— it seemed as though the whole world was swirling around him at a terrific speed. Bill, confused and bewildered, not knowing what had happened, let go of all the controls. But the instructor was on the job.

Soon the whirling ceased, and when Bill came to himself, Monteith had landed the plane on the airport.

"What happened?" asked Bill.

Monteith was laughing. "That was a spin—a tail spin—you held the stick back too long and she went into a tight spin. You see, Bill, when an aeroplane loses flying speed, or in flying terminology 'stalls', it is out of control until flying speed is regained. If this occurs at low altitudes, the consequence may be serious, or at least unfortunate. From the stall position, it is only a short step to the spin, which requires additional time and loss of altitude before sufficient speed for flight can be regained. An aeroplane may go into a spin from a variety of attitudes of flight. Most spins start from stalls, but it is possible to make certain types of aircraft enter spins without first completely stalling. A normal spin is accomplished by pulling the nose of the airplane up until it loses flying speed, causing it to stall. When the plane is in this position, it may be caused to start spinning by the application of either right or left rudder."

"Is that what I did?" interrupted Bill.

"Yes", said Monteith.

"Gee, I didn't know I applied either rudder."

"But you did", continued Monteith. "If this maneuver is executed intentionally at a sufficiently safe altitude, recovery ordinarily is simple. But the plane probably will lose 200 to 500 feet of altitude during process of recovery, and for this reason it is imperative that a safe altitude be reached before the spin is commenced. If a spin is entered into below a safe altitude, the plane may strike the ground before control is regained."

"Oh, I see why you went up so high to practice stalls—then you must have thought I would go into a spin."

"New students usually do the first few stalls they attempt", said Monteith. "In certain attitudes of flight a normal spin may be entered unintentionally. For instance, when a plane is banked beyond an angle of 45 degrees the rudder and elevator interchange functions. When in this position it is necessary to remove the rudder applied to enter the turn and perhaps to apply a slight amount of opposite rudder to keep the nose up. At the same time the stick is pulled farther back to hold the plane in the turn by the rudder effect of the elevators. If the rudder is left in the same position in which it was placed to enter the turn, it will cause the nose to drop after the plane banks at an angle of more than 45 degrees, as it acts as the elevator. The natural tendency of the pilot when the nose starts to drop is to pull back on the stick. This, however, merely serves to tighten the turn and lessen the flying speed. Such use of the stick, together with the bottom-rudder action, forces the plane into a spin.

"Numerous unintentional spins of this type occur when pilots not possessed of a great amount of experience are practicing maneuvers, such as figure eights and spirals. If they take place at altitudes below 800 feet, recovery before striking the ground is a matter for conjecture.

"A lack of co-ordination of controls, particularly during the first turn after take-off, is responsible for a number of spins occurring at low altitudes. Inexperienced pilots sometimes have a tendency to bank insufficiently on the first turn and to use an excessive amount of rudder. The 'skid' which results kills the flying speed, and the rudder already applied causes an unintentional spin, which, when occurring at a low altitude may result disastrously. It is chiefly on this account that flying instructors caution students to gain ample altitude before making the first turn.

"The crossed control spin is another type which is commonly entered unintentionally. This occurs when the pilot, in executing a bank, applies too much rudder in the direction of the turn, and attempts to correct it by applying opposite aileron. For example, in executing a right turn, right rudder and aileron are applied. After the desired amount of bank is obtained, the stick should be returned to neutral in order to keep the bank from increasing.

"If too much rudder has been applied, or the rudder effects start to reverse as the plane approaches the attitude of reversed control, there is a tendency on the part of some pilots to apply left aileron in order to correct the effective action of the rudder. With right rudder and left aileron, the plane controls then counteract each other, killing the forward speed and producing conditions which are conducive to a spin. Unfortunately, a fairly large proportion of mishaps result from unintentional spins at low altitudes. Prominent among accidents in this category are those resulting from lack of proper judgment in attempting to bank and turn too soon after taking off, trying to get back into the field shortly after the take-off, stretching the glide with engine off, and rudder turns with insufficient aileron."

"That must have been what happened to that plane in Long Beach that fell to the ground from 200 feet altitude?" Bill inquired.

"Yes, just that. His motor quit and he tried to turn back to the field without having sufficient altitude, thus overstretching the glide. It would have been better had he just nosed 'er down and continued straight ahead, regardless of what was in front of him.

"In a few cases abnormal or unconventional spins, from which recovery is difficult and sometimes impossible, occur in planes which are out of alignment due to twisted fuselages, tail surfaces, or improperly rigged wings. Planes which are licensed by the Department of Commerce are tested for spin characteristics at the time of initial approval of the aircraft type, and any undue spinning tendencies eliminated. The Department regulations which pertain to spin-testing require that aircraft recover from two, four, and six turn spins within a turn and half after the controls have been returned to neutral. These tests are conducted with the stabilizer set for cruising.

"The airplane submitted for test is usually a new one, and consequently rigged properly. While it is acknowledged that recovery will be slower with full negative stabilizer, or if the plane is improperly rigged, it is believed that under such conditions rapid recovery will be possible with opposite control because original recovery was tested with neutral controls. It is essential in view of these facts that aircraft be maintained in proper alignment in accordance with rigging diagrams furnished by the manufacturer, in order to preclude the possibility of unfavorable spin characteristics appearing."

"Oh", said Bill, "now I see why the Department of Commerce is so particular about inspecting the licensed airplanes every so often."

"Another type of spin, which, however, occurs only infrequently, is the so-called flat spin. In this type of spin, the plane when stalled remains in a flat position with the nose nearly level and rotates about a vertical axis, whereas in a normal spin the nose drops after the plane is stalled, and the plane rotates partially around its longitudinal axis. The degree of flatness influences the time needed for recovery. Flat spins usually occur in planes which are longitudinally unstable, and in which the center of gravity is located farther back than is normal, although this may not always be the case.

"Test pilots are inclined to add still another type of spin, known as the uncontrollable spin, which may or may not be flat, but from which it is impossible to recover on account of the design of the airplane and the direction of the air flow across the control surfaces. Abnormal spins, such as the flat spin and uncontrollable types, will only be encountered in experimental, newly designed planes, or those which have been allowed to get out of alignment due to improper inspection and maintenance. The pilot of a plane which is licensed by the Department of Commerce, carefully inspected at the required intervals and maintained in proper condition, need have little fear of spins in the abnormal class.

"Recovery from a spin normally is accomplished by neutralizing the elevator and rudder controls. In the early days of aviation it was necessary to push the stick ahead of neutral, centralize the rudder, and pull out of the resultant dive after attaining flying speed. Most modern types of aircraft will recover readily with the controls neutral, and acquire flying speed so quickly that excessive down elevator is not necessary. The application of opposite rudder ordinarily hastens recovery. The only point which should be borne in mind is that the rudder should be neutralized when the plane stops spinning in order to prevent it from spinning in the opposite direction. This will occur if the plane has not been nosed down enough to regain flying speed and the opposite rudder action has not been removed.

"Application of power, opposite aileron, or pumping the elevators may assist in recovery from abnormal spins, but no fixed rules can be established in this respect, as abnormal spins vary widely in their individual characteristics. In the case of a normal spin, application of power usually will hasten recovery. It is important that you know how to spin and how to accomplish recovery. You should also know the approximate altitude necessary for recovery in the particular plane you are flying, as such knowledge may be of material assistance in recovery from spins entered inadvertently at low altitudes.

"It is not necessary to caution the experienced flyer who, through long hours of experience, has learned that it is the conservative flyer who is the greatest credit to aviation. Such pilots constantly follow the few simple rules which guarantee safety of flight and do not need admonitions against careless flying. By their own careful flying practices they set examples which can be extremely beneficial to less experienced pilots who have not yet discovered that an airplane normally is safe but can be made extremely dangerous by recklessness in operation.

"I do not mean to convey the impression that acrobatic flying should be entirely taboo. It is believed that the experience gained from acrobatic flying in a suitable plane at safe altitudes in accordance with the Air Commerce Rules and Regulations, and with the pilot wearing a parachute, can be beneficial. But acrobatics at improper altitudes and at variance with the regulations can be hazardous both to the pilot and the spectators, as well as detrimental to the best interests of aviation. So that will be all today, Bill. Think over what I have told you and tomorrow we will take some more spins."

That night Bill dreamed of spins in everything. He even dreamed that he had descended into the swirling maelstrom of Edgar Allan Poe's story.

The next day, however, after going through three spins, Bill was quite able to kick the plane into and out of a spin. In the next two lessons he was given forced landings. The instructor would close the throttle at various altitudes and Bill would have to make an approach to the best landing place in that vicinity—this was to test his judgment in an emergency. But one day the practiced forced landing turned into a real forced landing. They were 3,000 feet up. The instructor closed the throttle and held his hand on it to keep Bill from opening it, thus conveying the thought that the motor had quit. Bill made a nice spiral and approach to a field, and just as the instructor was satisfied with the approach he opened the throttle to climb out, but the motor did not respond. In spiralling down, idling, the motor wasn't cleared, had loaded up, and so the instructor fooled himself—the motor backfired and quit for good. And Bill had to make a forced landing for true. After a good lecture about clearing the motor when spiralling down, they were off again.

Bill now had ten hours of flying. He thought he was a wonderful flyer. Today he was to start take-offs and landings.

When he arrived at the field, instead of starting the motor, Monteith carried him over to the railing fence, where they sat down for another lecture.

"Now, Bill", he started, "many of the mishaps which occur in aircraft operations, arise from difficulties encountered during take-offs. Except when unusual conditions cause complications, the maneuver of taking off is a comparatively simple one. However, in spite of this, accidents due to take-offs rank third in order of frequency.

"Practically without exception, the first precaution to be taken by the pilot in all cases should be to check the gasoline and oil supply personally, as there is no substitute for first-hand knowledge that the tanks are full. It should be seen that the fuel supply is sufficient to furnish a comfortable margin of safety in the event that the pilot runs into bad weather, or flies farther than he had intended.

"A second necessary precaution is to examine carefully the condition of the safety belt, seeing that it is properly secured and adjusted to fit snugly, but not so tight as to cause discomfort. Negligence in taking this precaution may mean the difference between severe injuries and none at all in the event of a mishap occurring while taking off. If the plane hits a depression, causing it to bounce, the pilot may be shaken enough so that he loses control temporarily, unless he is held firmly in position by his safety belt. Also, in the event the plane strikes some obstacle, or is caused to nose over through some unforeseen contingency, injuries may be inflicted upon the pilot through being thrown violently against the cowling or instrument board, or even out of the plane, if his safety belt does not hold him securely to his seat.

"All of the traditional precautions, such as the signals 'switch off' and 'contact' and the use of chocks under the wheels, should be observed in starting and warming the engine preparatory to taking off. The wheels should be blocked, even though the plane is equipped with brakes, as an added precaution against the plane starting forward suddenly and endangering persons or other aircraft in the vicinity. The engine should be warmed gradually until the oil temperature gauge shows that it has reached its normal operating temperature. It then should run with the throttle wide open long enough to see that it develops the proper ground revolutions per minute. Also, the pilot should check the oil pressure and see that the fuel valves are fully turned on and connected with the tank that is to be used first.

"If the spark has been retarded during the warming up period, it should be made certain that it is fully advanced before taking off. Also, the mixture control should be checked to see that it is in the proper position. In addition, the airman should check the position of the radiator shutter and cowling shutters and carburetor heaters, for the purpose of ascertaining whether they are properly adjusted in relation to atmospheric conditions. The stabilizer should be set for balance at cruising speed. And, as a last precaution, the pilot should move the control stick and rudder in order to check the operation of the control system and surfaces, seeing that their operation is normal.

"Before starting to taxi for the take-off position, the position of other planes on the ground and in the air should be observed, to preclude any possibility of collision. The taxi should be made down the side of the field to prevent interference with traffic. In taxying, the throttle should be opened sufficiently to maintain an even speed, which should be only fast enough to maintain control while on the ground. The plane should not be taxied by intermittent bursts of the throttle, as this puts an unnecessary strain on both the plane and the motor. Taxying is not a maneuver which ordinarily would be thought of as a dangerous operation; yet accidents have occurred, practically all preventable, which were due directly to a lack of proper attention on the part of the pilot. Accidents of this type have included collisions with other aircraft while taxying during landings or take-offs, as well as collisions with boundary lights or field markers.

"If the engine has been allowed to idle for several minutes, between the time of testing at full throttle on the line and the time of placing the plane in position of take-off, it again should be checked at full throttle to make certain that it has not loaded up or fouled a plug. Before starting the take-off, the pilot should glance at the ailerons to see that they are in the neutral position. When in position for the take-off, the throttle should be advanced to full open position and the tail should be raised gradually by forward pressure on the control stick. This is the only time in flying when force is actually necessary on the control stick, due to the plane's not having attained sufficient speed to permit the air stream to exert its normal amount of force on the tail surfaces.

"The pilot should maintain a straight course during take-off, correcting any tendencies to turn right or left by pressure on the rudder pedals. He should not seesaw the rudder, but, rather, should anticipate the tendency to deviate from a straight course and correct by pressure or slight movement on the control. The plane should be held at a level altitude until flying speed is attained, at which time it either will leave the ground of its own accord, or in response to slight backward pressure on the control stick.

"In the actual take-off, with the less experienced pilot, there is often a tendency to allow the plane to drift across wind, due to failure to hold it into the wind. This tendency may result in the plane's getting into the path of other planes taking off, or drifting into obstructions on the boundaries of the field. Also, there is the possibility of the pilot's completely losing control due to the plane drifting sidewise as it gets into the air. If the tail is too high during the take-off, the plane will develop a tendency to bounce on the wheels as soon as any appreciable amount of speed has been attained, and if the field is rough and the plane strikes a depression, there is the possibility of nosing over. If the tail is not raised high enough, the plane will leave the ground in a stalled attitude, which will be accompanied by sluggish action of the controls.

"The nature of the surface of the airport will influence the method of taking off to a great degree. On a hard surface or runway field it is relatively easy to hold the plane straight, and flying speed can be attained quickly. On a muddy or plowed field, or one covered with high grass or snow, it is necessary to hold the tail down to prevent the plane's nosing over while it is gathering flying speed. This also means that it will take longer to attain flying speed, making it absolutely necessary to use all available space. If the field is muddy, and difficulty is experienced in getting off, it may be advantageous to let some of the air out of the tires, to enable the plane to start rolling. In connection with take-offs from rough or soft fields, the feel of the plane as it gathers speed, or fails to do so, will indicate to the pilot familiar with that particular plane its proper attitude and the nicety of control movement necessary to ease it into the air at the exact moment when it is ready to fly.

"In taking off from small fields, accidents have occurred due to excessive haste on the part of the pilot in attempting to get the plane into the air. In some cases, pilots have stalled the plane completely after take-off by having tried to get into the air quickly. The first essentials in taking off from a small field are to attain sufficient flying speed, hold the plane level during the take-off and take advantage of all available field space. Even if there are obstructions directly ahead of the pilot, he has a much better chance of clearing them if he has attained sufficient flying speed than if he has attempted to get into the air too quickly.

"In the event that a cross-wind take-off is unavoidable, the pilot should counteract for drift by the use of the rudder, and a slight amount of aileron, in order to maintain a straight course while leaving the ground. The first turn in all cases should be made into the wind in preference to down wind.

"As soon as the plane gets into the air the stick should be pulled back sufficiently to assume a normal climbing attitude, which should be maintained until enough altitude has been obtained to make the first turn well outside the boundaries of the airport. This altitude may be anywhere between 300 and 800 feet, depending upon the airplane and the type of terrain adjoining the airport. Excessively steep climbs on the take-off should at all times be avoided, due to the likelihood of the plane's being unable to maintain flying speed should the engine cut out. Neither should the airplane be held down below its normal climbing attitude since attainment of altitude is desirable in order to have sufficient room in which to maneuver in case of emergency.

"The consensus of opinion based on long experience in the case of engine failure on the take-off, or at low altitudes, dictates that the plane should be landed straight ahead regardless of obstructions, or, at the most, only shallow turns should be made in order to avoid obstacles and land in a clear space. In no event should the pilot make a nose high turn in order to get back into the airport, as the maneuver of turning without sufficient forward speed may send the plane downward entirely out of control, while in landing straight forward the pilot usually will be able to maintain some degree of control.

"The mixture control should not be moved until sufficient altitude has been gained. If the control is moved during the take-off, it may cause the mixture to become lean, with a resulting coughing or spitting of the engine, or it may cause the engine to quit entirely. The possibility of structural failure of the airplane, or failure of the engine, can be almost entirely eliminated by proper inspection before the plane leaves the ground.

"A pilot was forced to make a landing on a hillside due to some minor trouble. After making the necessary adjustment, which required only a short time, he prepared to take-off. There was a slight wind blowing across the slope, and it appeared advisable to take off into the wind and stall the plane off the field, as there seemed a danger of nosing over because of a long second growth of grass which covered the ground. In taking off, the pilot had to pass close to a fence at the left of the field, and in so doing neglected looking often enough to the right where there were some trees. The plane veered downhill, and the pilot saw the trees in his path too late to avoid them. The plane had just gotten into the air when it hit the trees.

"In an analysis of this case the apparent errors resolve themselves into two classes—technique and judgment. The pilot evinced poor technique in not holding the plane on a straight course to avoid the obstacles. There was also the added possibility that he became impatient and stalled the plane into the air too quickly. Furthermore, he apparently looked out from only one side of the plane after starting the take-off. The error of judgment was that of not taking off downhill, as the cross wind, or even a tail wind, would have been more than compensated for by the incline of the hill.

"An error on the part of the pilot was also involved in another instance: A normal take-off commenced in dead air at a field situated at an altitude of nearly 3,000 feet. The plane rose twenty feet, but even when it was being leveled off to gain speed, it settled slowly to the ground and struck some low scrub trees. The engine functioned perfectly throughout, but the plane apparently would not take off properly at this altitude in dead air. The pilot's error in this case was that he failed to consider that the decreased atmospheric density due to altitude means decreased lift, and that consequently increased speed is necessary to obtain the required amount of lift for normal flight.

"In another case the pilot started to take off into the north with a west wind blowing. When the plane had reached an altitude of about thirty feet, a gust of wind from the west lifted the left wing to an angle of about twenty-five degrees. Full stick control was immediately applied by the pilot to level the plane laterally, but the wind had the greater advantage, and the plane drifted toward trees on the side of the field. Still keeping the controls in position to right the plane, the pilot finally managed to bank to the left about fifteen feet from the trees and landed with minor damages to the fuselage and under carriage of the plane. Circumstances in this case were not such as to be beyond the control of the pilot. The error occurred in stalling the plane off the ground without adequate flying speed. When this happens it is always accompanied by slow response of the plane to the controls. This instance was purely a matter of flying technique."

With the lecture over, Bill was showed how to start the motor, warm it up, inspect all instruments, and prepare for the take-off. With throttle open and stick pushed forward the plane roared down the field. The farther it went the lighter it seemed to get and the less force was necessary to apply to the stick until finally the plane lifted from the ground, but not until it had curved from one end of the field to the other. Bill tried it several times, but could not hold it straight on the take-off. His landings were pretty good, his approaches better—yes, he could level off and set the plane down on three points fine. But it took three solid hours of take-offs and landings. After he had completed his thirteenth hour, it looked as though he just could not make the plane go straight on the ground. His air work was fine. The instructor had bawled him out for the "umteenth" time.

"I guess you are a hopeless case; I don't see how in the world you got such good grades in your other aeronautical studies. You are the dumbest flyer I ever met. You'll never learn to fly", said Mr. Monteith after they were down, and he even went home without saying good night.

Bill was heart-broken. He had told all his friends he was flying, and they all expected to go out to see him, and now it seemed as though the instructor had given him up.

Well, he determined to fly that ship the next day or tear it up. He didn't sleep that night at all. Next day he was sitting in the cockpit long before the instructor arrived, trying to figure out why he could not take off straight. His trouble was in manipulating the rudder. He had been pressing the rudder against the small part of the foot and against the heel. This time he decided to use the toe of the shoe instead of the middle part.

Presently Mr. Monteith arrived. "Well, we'll try it once more before I give you up", he said to Bill. Of course this statement made Bill's heart feel as heavy as stone. All his hopes about to be shattered if he didn't fly that ship today.

"Now, remember", said Monteith just before taking off, "you're trying to make a big job out of this taking off, and it's a whole lot easier than landing or flying.

Just hold even pressure on each rudder pedal. If it starts to the left, press the right rudder gradually. O.K. Let's go."

Glancing around to ascertain whether the road was clear, and to see if there were any ships in the air, Bill opened the throttle. Down the field the ship sped just as straight as possible for it to go. This amazed as well as gratified Bill. What had happened? He hastened for a landing in order to try another take-off, which he made with equal success. Can you beat that? What caused it? He has never been able to ascertain definitely, unless, as he figured, his toes were more sensitive than the other part of his feet. Anyway he made four perfect take-offs. His landings had been fairly good for quite some time.

The last time he landed, the instructor told him to taxi all the way back to the end of the field. When he had turned the ship around for another take-off, the instructor slowly got out of the plane. He readjusted the stabilizer, looked to see that Bill's belt was properly secured, then very calmly said, "Now, Bill, I want you to take off, circle the field twice at 1,000 feet, and then land. Be careful and watch out for other planes; if you overshoot, go on around and try it again. There's no hurry."

Bill, greatly surprised, said, "Alone?"

"Yes, alone! You can do it all right."

This was rather surprising, for only yesterday Mr. Monteith told Bill he would never make a flyer, and today he was letting him solo. Funny business, this flying. The instructor did that to keep Bill from developing overconfidence in himself.

Without another word Bill opened the throttle and soon was in the air. What a thrill! Up in the air all alone! A thousand thoughts passed through his mind. But he was quite at home, and why shouldn't he be? He knew how to get out of the most difficult maneuvers, and he had had thirteen hours in the air before solo-ing—thanks to Mr. Monteith.

Around the field at 1,000 feet and then land, Bill thought. The first time around he made himself quite at home looking over the side of the ship at those on the ground watching him. He even waved. Yes, he's getting too smart right at the start. He's coming in now for a landing. Everybody is out of the hangars and shops watching Bill solo—he's 'way too high—he'll land 'way out in the weeds on the rough ground—probably he'll nose over, break a propeller, probably the ship will catch fire. He is side-slipping, but he's too high, even at that. The instructor is watching him very calmly. But Bill, too, has noticed that he cannot make the field from that height, and so he gives her the gun and goes around again, and Monteith heaves a sigh of relief.

He's shooting again for a landing, but this time in an effort not to overshoot he falls 'way short of the mark, and endeavoring to make the field, he gains too much speed, due to opening the throttle. He realizes this, and again gives her the gun to go around again. By this time it has become quite interesting to the on-lookers. Many asked, can't he get down? And many other silly questions. But his third approach was perfect. He glided in and made a perfect three-point land-ing, right on the circle. And now his chest did stick out. Taxying back to the end of the field he turned around for another take-off, but was told by Monteith that that was all for the day, whereupon he informed Mr. Monteith that he still had ten minutes of his time left, enough for another round. But the wise instructor realized that the good landing had probably gone to his head, and another flight that day might be dis-astrous.

Next day about twenty-five of Bill's friends were out to the field to see him fly solo. Mr. Monteith saw them, and so Bill didn't get a chance to solo that day.

"Nothing doing, Bill; you haven't enough time to start showing off yet in front of anyone." And Bill only flew solo on days that none of his friends were around. He soon learned to keep them away.

The next ten hours were spent preparing to take the private pilot's examination. And hence within three weeks the instructor flew Bill over to Mines Field for the test.

The first thing he had to do was to take a written examination on Air Commerce Rules and Regulations and Air Traffic Laws—ten questions on each. And then the flight test.

The Department of Commerce inspector instructed Bill to go up and make a spot landing from straight approach at an altitude of 500 feet; then land within 500 feet in front of a designated mark; then from an altitude of 1500 feet make a 360 degree turn with engine throttled and land 500 feet from the mark. Then from an altitude of 1200 feet to make a 180 degree turn with motor throttled and land as usual. Next he was to execute a series of three gentle and three steep figure eight turns around pylons 1,000 feet apart at 800 and then 1,000 feet altitude respectively. The last maneuver was to spiral down from 2,000 feet with engine throttled and make a spot landing within the mark. Of course Bill had no difficulty whatsoever in doing these maneuvers, thanks to Mr. Monteith. And so he was the happiest person in the world when he was given his PRIVATE PILOT'S LICENSE.

CHAPTER V

THE BUSINESS MANAGER ARRIVES

As before indicated, we often find Bill sitting in the president's office, asking advice. One day while they were thus conversing, Mr. Warren inquired of Bill whether he intended that Rogers and Wooten should become instructors in his first group of ten.

Learning that those were Bill's intentions, Mr. Warren said: "Then you have made your first mistake. Now don't misunderstand me. Rogers and Wooten are very fine fellows and very conscientious, but you see they are having great difficulty with their studies. They have not enough education. They'll make good mechanics under someone, but they will never be able to pass a written examination on airplane or engine mechanics."

"Yes," said Bill, "I have discovered that, and I have been wondering just what to do, as we don't care to waste the $700 spent on their courses. They were such good automobile mechanics in Chicago that I never even dreamed about inquiring into their educational qualifications."

And so the next day we find Bill writing a letter to Neely, telling him that their first $700 had been blown up, temporarily anyhow, as neither Rogers nor Wooten would be able to be used in the first group of ten, who must be able to instruct in his or her particular line, but he stated that later on they would make good workers or helpers. And thus Bill suffered his first setback toward winning his bet with Braddan.

All the airports and air schools were buzzing with comment about the coming National Air Races, to be held at Mines Field in August, 1929. Warren School

students were particularly interested because they had
been given charge of the field and the events. Several
squadrons of Army and Navy planes were to take part
in the races and events, as would most of the cele-
brated flyers of the country. On the opening day of
the air races, Bill was on the emergency truck. Some
job, he thought. He certainly felt very important.
There was a rehearsal. The big siren blew, (it could be
heard for more than a mile) denoting an accident, and
across the field the speedy Moreland truck dashed with
block and tackle and all kinds of tools, ropes, crowbars,
etc. Bill stood ready to be pressed into any service
necessary. There were three other students on the
truck. A nice job for those boys. All they had to do
was to cruise up and down the field before the grand-
stand of a hundred thousand people. Bill was therefore fortunate to be able to keep in contact with everything going on.

The "Three Sea Hawks," the Navy's best, stole the
show. Led by Lieut. Tomlinson, Bill saw his first real
exhibition of acrobatics—barrel rolls in formation,
loops, spins, power dives, everything imaginable. "The
Three Musketeers," the Army's best, tried in vain to
outmaneuver the Navy flyers, but to no avail. The
straffing of the Army and Navy planes in formations
of twenty-seven each was a wonderful sight. Al Wil-
son in his old pusher type plane came up for his share
of the applause. The smoke screens were also thrilling
sights. Bill was certainly getting first-hand experience
for his own future flying exhibitions, for these demonstrations were of the very best. The races were quite
a feature. Near the end of the week, competition was
so keen that Lieut. Williams, of the "Three Musketeers", went to his death, stunting low. Bill was one
of the first to reach the wreck of his plane. Then Col.
Charles Lindbergh, who had just arrived, took Lieut.
Williams' place leading the "Three Musketeers."

Quite fortunately for our Bill, he was the only colored fellow out on the field—Rogers and Wooten were working during the day and attending school at night. But toward the end of the week, while the truck was cruising along in front of the grandstands, an acquaintance of Bill's, named William Browne, called Bill. Bill jumped from the truck, and after talking to Browne awhile learned that he had a friend named Walter Swaggerty who was on the outside but didn't have the dollar admission price. Browne asked Bill to loan his pass to Swaggerty, which he did, very reluctantly, however. After a short while Bill ran across both Browne and Swaggerty, who had not only gained admission to the grandstands, but, with the aid of Bill's pass, had come out on the field where only the

WALTER SWAGGERTY (at left) MINES FIELD, LOS ANGELES

contestants and workers were supposed to be. Browne was taking a picture of Swaggerty standing by one of the contesting planes. Bill was introduced to Mr. Swaggerty, who said he was the only Negro licensed pilot in America, and that he was an entrant in the "Dole Hawaii Race." When asked how far he went across, he explained that the fellow he was to fly with didn't get his ship ready in time, so they never started.

Bill told Swaggerty of his future plans, stating

that if he was a licensed pilot, he could see no reason why he should not join the movement. So Swaggerty agreed to cast his lot with the group immediately. When Bill asked to see his license he explained that he had left it at home in his other clothes, but assured Bill that he would bring it with him the following Sunday when he would talk over the plans; but to this day Bill has never seen him again. However, the following week, an article appeared in a local Negro newspaper, stating that Swaggerty, flying Monocoup No. 88, was the only Negro pilot attending the National Air Races, winning several events. It happened that this Monocoup No. 88 was the plane Swaggerty was standing in front of when Browne snapped his picture the day Bill ran into them at Mines Field.

A short time after the National Air Races in Los Angeles, the Warren School was again honored by having charge of the field at San Diego when Lindbergh Field was dedicated. Another great crowd, with plenty of hair-raising stunts, and Bill was again fortunate enough to get his old job on the service truck. Great experience he was getting. Surely he would some day be able to direct a big colored air show.

A year had passed. Bill was progressing wonderfully. He and two other white fellows (as he would often say to his friends) had rebuilt a Waco 9 from start to finish, and the Department of Commerce had licensed it. The last I heard of it, it was still flying. He had just commenced his navigation training under Lieut. Commander Williams.

One day, like a bolt of thunder out of the clouds, Bill received a telegram, which read as follows:

"Arriving Southern Pacific tomorrow.
Meet me 4 P.M.

Burrell Neely."

Well, of all things! Bill still had five months to go to school, but the next day he was on time at the railroad station.

"Hello, Pal," greeted Bill, as Neely was seen surging out of the crowd.

"THE BUSINESS MANAGER HAS ARRIVED. I thought it was high time we started getting our business organized", was Neely's reply.

"Welcome, old top; I say as much", returned Bill.

"How are you progressing in school?"

"Fine."

"Good! California certainly is a beautiful place. I've never enjoyed a train ride any better than that through Southern California. I never saw so many oranges before in all my life, and I understand that California flying weather is the best we have in the country."

"So you have been reading up on flying in California, have you?"

"Well, you see it's like this," Neely continued, "my business is AIR, and I am full of my subject."

They both had a hearty laugh and were soon on their way to Bill's home on the West Side.

Outside of visiting his brother and an uncle here, it was not long before Neely was giving all his time to the organization of the business. He had a plan all worked out, that he went into discussion with Bill about. Neely argued that the organization should be composed of an "Executive Group" and an "Operations Group": the Executive Group to be composed of twelve directors incorporated into a company; the Operations Group should consist of ten as originally planned, each of whom should be trained in one particular branch of aeronautics.

Bill agreed with this plan, but they differed when the matter of the personnel of the Executive Group came up. Neely argued that he could interest ten Los Angeles people who had enough finance to sponsor the movement, Neely and Bill to complete the twelve. Bill, on the other hand, argued that as long as the movement was to be national in scope the twelve directors should be chosen from all parts of the United States, and that they should be such people as Mr. Vann, Editor of the Pittsburgh Courier; Mr. Abbott, Editor of the Chicago Defender; Mr. Moton, of Tuskeegee; Mrs. Nannie Burroughs, and other equally prominent and well known persons. With such people as leaders, a wholesale interest in aviation among members of the group would only be a matter of time; such a lineup, according to Bill, would certainly be inspiration enough, and these men and women could certainly map out a plan of organization that would lead the Negroes to commercial success in the aviation industry.

Burrell Neely

But Neely won the argument, because both figured it would take too long to reach these people, and then, probably, they could not be approached on the subject, so he set out to get his Executive Group in Los Angeles. His first step was to ascertain from the Corporation Commissioner just what was necessary. He found out that he must have at least $10,000 to incorporate, and with this plan he started the list with $1,000.

He then put down Bill's name, asking him how much he would invest. "Three thousand dollars in cash", Bill replied.

"And something not in cash?" asked Neely.

"I paid $700 already for those two boys' courses in school. What about that?" said Bill.

"What I am interested in now is $10,000 in cash to meet the Commissioner's demand. Then, after incorporating, I will have the company issue you and me stock for our expenditures to date. Well, $4,000 is not a bad start. It should be easy to raise the other $6,000 here. I'm going to canvass the well-to-do's, but before doing that we should open an office and select a temporary name. Shall we decide definitely on your previous suggestion, Bill, for a name—Bessie Coleman Aero Clubs?"

"We would at least be doing something that Negroes generally do not do," answered Bill.

"What's that?" said Neely, starting up.

"We would be honoring a pioneer who I think well deserves the honor."

"Granted."

In a few days Neely had opened offices at 1423 West Jefferson Boulevard. As Bill was still in school, and Neely's business for the most part was out of the office, he hired a stenographer. One day Bill came in from school just as Neely had dictated his first letter in the office.

"You're just in time, Bill. I've just dictated a letter to the Department of Commerce inquiring as to Negro licensed pilots and mechanics throughout America. I thought this very important at this time, for if there happened to be any licensed Negroes we could write them, and give them a chance to join your Operations Group. I repeat again that this is a big thing, and co-operation must be the slogan. The day of rampant individualism has passed. Business institutions that are most successful are those that combine the greatest possible co-operative spirit with private initiative. If the Negro is ever to enter the business field with profit he must lay aside personalities and submerge them in collective effort. I hope you realize this, Bill, and that you will ever try to keep this standard aloft in this organization, for, this being a new field leaves many openings for individuals to endeavor to branch off alone for personal aggrandizement and personal honors.. There is, however, no gain to be made by preaching racial collectivism and then attempting to center it behind individual direction. It is only as the race at large participates, not only in the upbuilding of our institutions, but in their active management and direction, that we can hope for success. Co-operation must become more than an 'empty phrase', it must be made a reality."

"You're right, Neely," said Bill. "I think we have a wonderful business manager."

Several days later a reply from the Department of Commerce read as follows:

DEPARTMENT OF COMMERCE
OFFICE OF THE
ASSISTANT SECRETARY FOR AERONAUTICS
WASHINGTON

Bessie Coleman Aero Clubs,
1423 West Jefferson Blvd.,
Los Angeles, Calif.
Gentlemen: Attention: Burrell Neely

Receipt is acknowledged of your letter of November 3.

This Department is not in a position to recommend flying instructors. The reason for such policy is obvious.

At this time we are not aware of any negro who holds a commercial pilot's license or a mechanic's license.

There is, of course, nothing in the Air Commerce Regulations which would prohibit the holding of such license.

Very truly yours,
JESSIE W. LANKFORD,
Chief, Licensing Section.

RSP/es

"Yes, it certainly is a wide open field, and we really are pioneers in our race," said Neely to Bill, after reading the letter, "and that letter should be published to let the Negroes in America know just where we stand.

I'm going to send this letter to the Associated Negro Press."

And so the following week this letter appeared in Negro papers all over America; and well that it did—it created quite a sensation. Many letters regarding this write-up were received at the office. The following week, there was a write-up in the California Eagle by Artis Ward, who had been the partner of "Ace" Foreman on their projected cross country flight. Ward's write-up stated that he was a licensed mechanic (although he failed to state his license number), and he also stated that he knew a Negro commercial flyer in Ames, Iowa, named Herman Banning. He then attacked the Bessie Coleman Aero Clubs for having such an article printed. This attack by Ward was quite absurd, and became more so when, in a few days, a letter came to the office from James Herman Banning in Ames, Iowa, stating that he was a flyer interested in the Bessie Coleman program, but that he was not licensed at that time, and had not been for several months—his license having expired.

Bill answered Banning's letter, telling him of the organization's plans, and extending him an invitation to join the group. They also received a letter from Dr. A. Porter Davis, of Kansas, the flying physician who owned his own plane. The proposition was submitted to him also.

A letter was received from a Capt. E. C. McVey, enclosing his picture showing himself attired in boots and spurs and a Sam Browne belt, but his letter didn't sound as if he had any knowledge of aeronautics, so further communication with him was dropped.

Publication of this letter also brought many visitors to the office, one of the first being a very clean cut young man, tall, handsome, and straightforward.

"Gentlemen", he said, as he walked into the office.

"Neely is my name," said our alert business manager quickly, greeting the young man at the door with extended hand.

"Irvin Wells is my name", replied the visitor.

"Mr. Wells, shake hands with Mr. William Brown, my partner."

After acknowledging the introduction, Mr. Wells spoke of having seen the letter in the paper, remarking that he was certainly glad to see some one of the race take the initiative in the aviation field. He also stated that he had wanted to learn to fly for the past two years.

After Neely explained his proposition, it took no thinking it over for Wells. It was just what he had been thinking about for some time. Neely then went over Wells' educational qualifications, and pronounced him qualified and eligible for either the Executive or Operations Group, or both.

Wells replied as follows: "I'm most interested in flying, but I would like to get in on everything as much as possible. I don't know yet what your financial requirements are, but I can spare $300 cash now, and more later on, to be used as you see fit." And so Wells became the third member of the Executive and Operations Groups.

Next day, William Browne, the fellow who induced Bill to allow Swaggerty the use of his pass at Mines Field, stepped into the office. He also had read the letter, and stated that he would like to become an airplane mechanic. After much questioning, Neely decided to give Browne a course in airplane mechanics and train him for the Operations Group. That same day Oliver Betts, a newspaper man with wide and influential connections, stated that he would like to become a member of the Executive Group. He further stated that he was unable to invest any money, but that he felt that his acquaintance and influence with the press was worth something to the organization. Neely felt the same way about it. So a contract was drawn with Oliver Betts, providing that he should be in the Executive Group, that he should see that the organization was advertised as extensively as possible in Negro newspapers, that he would cover all exhibitions with proper write-ups, and that all cuts, mats, pictures, etc., necessary for these write-ups, should be given the organization at cost. The organization in turn was to issue him $1,000 worth of stock after it had incorporated.

Another young man attracted by the publication of the letter was not interested in flying, but was interested in the progress of the Negro in aviation. He was signed up with the Executive Group. Edward Graham, as he was named, invested $300.

A young lady, Miss Corona White, who impressed Neely very much with her businesslike manner and ideas, became a member of the Executive Group. She invested $200. It was later discovered that she was a cousin to Bill.

Neely was indeed working fast and hard. He brought in another man, named William Penson, an elderly man with much experience in advertising, road shows, etc. He was also named to the Executive Group and invested $500.

In a couple of days, Bill was handed a notice from Neely, as were all the other members of the Executive Group. This notice informed them that the first meeting of the incorporators would be held and temporary officers selected.

The important matters discussed at this meeting were the completion of the Executive and Operations Groups and the subsequent training of the future operators. Everybody was present but Oliver Betts. It was disclosed that the Executive Group had seven of the desired twelve members, and that $5,300 had been invested, including $4,000 invested by Neely and Bill. This was not so promising, especially since the training of the Operations Group could not start until a plane was purchased, and any decent plane at that time would cost at least $3,500.

A few days later, James Herman Banning, from Ames, Iowa, arrived to join the group. Banning had over 250 hours of flying to his credit, but due to inactivity had let his license expire. He had learned to fly in 1924, having been taught by an Army officer, friend of the family in Iowa. So plans were immediately taken under consideration to purchase a plane in order that Banning might get the necessary hours to reinstate his license, and help carry on the training of the others in the group. He was immediately designated Chief Pilot.

THE EXECUTIVE GROUP
Left to right: William Penson, Burrell Neely, Ed. Graham, Mrs. Susie Hancock, Miss Corona White, Harry LaVette

A young lady, Mrs. Florence Reeves, soon became a member of the Operations Group, as did William H. Johnson, who was formerly one of "Ace" Foreman's students. Two other young fellows were chosen, Wesley Cotton and Leo Walker.

The Operations Group was then ready to start training.

Bill was designated Navigator and Banning, Pilot. The others would have to be trained along different lines. However, there was a certain amount of general training that each would be given by Bill, before they would be sent to school to specialize. All were to take up flying under Banning. Again we find Bill with a full program, instructing the group in aerodynamics, navigation, meteorology, theory of flight, aircraft instruments, and air commerce rules and regulations. He conducted these classes at night from 7:30 to 10:30, and continued in the Warren College during the day. In the meantime the office was besieged by outsiders who wanted to join the classes.

Bill was quite happy, for he saw visions of a group of ten trained aeronauts flying to Chicago to see Rev. Braddan "pay off."

But, alas, there is many a slip between the cup and the lip. A letter from Miss Theodore in Cleveland notified the group that she was preparing to entrain for Los Angeles to join them. Things looked fine for the Operations Group, but Neely was having trouble with his Executive Group. Several weeks of appointments and disappointments with the supposed-to-be-well-to-do's in town, inviting them to elaborately laid dinners, lectures, smokers, etc., without result, made Neely quite a disgusted man.

"I can't understand it," he said at one of the incorporators' meetings. "I haven't been able to interest a single person further in the Executive Group. And we can't incorporate until we have the desired capital. I have interviewed hundreds of people, believe it or not, all of whom state that we have a wonderful proposition, but something had just happened, causing them to be financially unable to invest. Our expense is going on daily, thus diminishing what we have. Something must be done to stir up interest anew."

And so they voted to purchase an airplane for $3,500, an American Eagle. This caused great enthusiasm to be manifested among members of the Operations Group. They were all ready to begin flying, and there was much discussion in the office of Lyster and

Jones, medical examiners for the Department of Commerce, when seven Negro boys and girls applied for student permits. The students were certainly proud to be flying. They just could not keep Wesley Cotton and Leo Walker, the younger of the group, from walking around the streets with their flying apparel on. Neely said he was sitting in church one morning enjoying the service when, right in the middle of the sermon, he noticed all eyes turn toward the door. Looking around, he saw Leo Walker enter the church with his helmet and goggles on and walk half way down the aisle before removing them.

These students were so jealous of their positions that it led to much trouble. Florence Reeves, who was a very adept student, progressing most amazingly in her ground work, especially navigation, and doing fine in her flying too, was so wrapped up in the work that when the news got out that another young lady was en route to join the group, she, listening to the usual "Black Dispatch," understood that the young lady was coming to replace her. She was so upset that she issued an ultimatum to Neely, stating that no one was going to replace her and that she would break up the whole works first. Of course this came as a streak of lightning to Neely, who didn't even know the false rumor was out. He had spoken several times about Miss Theodore's coming, but had not said she was going to replace anyone.

Neely was a good business manager, full of new ideas. A few days later he brought a Chicago Defender into the office and told Bill to read the article about Oscar Depriest, only Negro Congressman, coming to Los Angeles.

"Well, that's fine, I'll go hear him", said Bill, after reading the article.

"Is that all you get out of that article?" asked Neely.

"I don't understand you," replied Bill.

"That article is of vast importance to the Bessie Coleman Aero Clubs," continued Neely. "We'll reach persons with capital then."

"How?" asked Bill.

"The day that Depriest arrives, you and Banning will circle over the railroad station, and then lead the welcoming procession of automobiles up Central Avenue to the Dunbar Hotel where Depriest will stop. On the plane we will paint in large letters, 'Oscar Depriest.' Mrs. Reeves and I will greet Depriest at the station, and we'll have Mrs. Reeves, all in her flying togs, extend an invitation to him to a plane christening in his honor. At the christening ceremony, Banning will take the Congressman up for a ride and, Oh, boy! talk about publicity—everybody will read about it, and I'll make all the contacts necessary to complete the Executive Group."

"Wonderful idea", said Bill. "Without a good business manager we would be sunk."

The following week the white newspapers carried an article stating that the Bessie Coleman Aero Clubs were to christen their new plane "Oscar Depriest" at a ceremony at the Lincoln Airport. The next day Neely rushed into the office out of breath—"Well, I'm getting results already," he said. "I want you to go with me tonight, Bill. I received a phone call from a lady who read of the coming event. An interview with her proved that she is very much interested in the progress of the Negro youth in aviation. She formerly taught school at Prairie View College, and her daughter married Booker T. Washington, Jr. Her name is Mrs. Hancock, and she will have $1,000 for us tonight as her investment for a seat on the Executive Board, providing we let her christen the plane. I promised her that I would let her christen the plane."

"Good work, Neely; it is a pleasure to work with one as far-seeing as you are," said Bill.

And so that night Mrs. Hancock was made a member of the Executive Group. They soon named Mrs. Hancock the mother of the club, because she was quite elderly—although she would never tell her age. She often stated that the happiest moment of her life would be when the group moved out on its tour, as she would feel that she had contributed something to the development of the Negro race.

The office was quite a busy place that day, as on the morrow the Congressman would arrive. Several visitors were at the office, among them two young ladies who had been frequent visitors at both the office and the field when the group was training—Mesdames Marie Dickerson and Mable Norman. Just then Leo Walker rushed into the office out of breath, and interrupted Neely's conversation with Mrs. Dickerson.

"Mrs. Reeves is going to throw us down tomorrow," he said.

"What do you mean?" asked Neely.

Walker continued—"She said there was another girl on the way here to take her place, and so she was not going to let you all use her for a tool until this girl came. Said she would throw a cog in the wheel first. She is not going to show up at the station when Depriest arrives tomorrow."

This statement took Neely and Bill off their feet, and before anything was said, Mrs. Dickerson broke the silence by saying that she wished she could take Mrs. Reeves' place on the morrow. An idea struck Neely. He told Mrs. Dickerson and Mrs. Norman to be dressed in flying suits and be on hand to take Mrs. Reeves' place in event she did not show up. He also decided to take Mrs. Dickerson as an alternate in the group in case Mrs. Reeves or Miss Theodore didn't make it. But this decision really started trouble.

The next day at the appointed hour, Bill and Banning flew the Oscar Depriest over the S. P. Station. Notwithstanding the fact that the Department of Commerce rules prohibit flying lower than 2,000 feet, under such conditions, Bill could plainly see a large crowd at the station and knew exactly when the Congressman came out of the station, for the crowd swayed backward and forward and milled about like so many ants. Presently the procession of automobiles crept slowly down Central Avenue, and the Oscar Depriest led the procession, executing S turns, 720 degree turns, and vertical banks in order not to get too far ahead of the slow-moving autos. At the hotel the procession stopped and another crowd assembled, while the Congressman paused a while and looked up at the plane bearing his name. Neely told Bill later that at

MRS. SUSIE HANCOCK CHRISTENS THE "OSCAR DEPRIEST"

that time he was showing the Congressman his name.

"And what do you think, Bill, Mrs. Reeves really didn't show up at the station," said Neely to Bill that night. "We'll stop this right now. She's through. Put Mrs. Dickerson in her place immediately. You know we must run this business, and not let the business run us."

"Too bad," said Bill. "We've given Mrs. Reeves several hours flying and several weeks of ground instruction; to have to go over all that ground is a loss of time and money; and furthermore she is exception-

THE "DEPRIEST" PARTY WATCHES THE "CHRISTENING"
Left to right—Mrs. Nellie V. Conner, Los Angeles; Madam Wyatt, Chicago; Mrs. Tommy Miles, Los Angeles; Mrs. Oscar Depriest; Mrs. Hussey, sister of Congressman Depriest

ally good and makes a wonderful appearance—she's an awfully good looking brown skin girl, you know."

"A wonderful appearance she made today—no appearance at all. Bill, we can't tolerate anything like that. We might as well stop the whole works."

And so Mrs. Reeves was scratched off the list and Mrs. Dickerson voted to replace her—another setback in Bill's race to win his bet from Rev. Braddan.

The following day the christening ceremony was held. Neely introduced Bill to explain the purpose of the organization. He then introduced Mrs. Hancock, who christened the plane "Oscar Depriest" amid the cheers of the crowd. Mr. J. B. Bass then introduced the Congressman, who delivered a most inspiring address. Among other things, he said he was proud to see the Negro taking steps to learn aviation, and that the citizens of Los Angeles should see to it that the Bessie Coleman Aero Clubs went over in a big way. After introducing Mrs. Depriest and the congressional party, J. Herman Banning carried Depriest for his first ride with a Negro pilot.

CHAPTER VI

THE ADVANCE TRIP

Three weeks passed. Training of the Operations Group was progressing wonderfully. The Bessie Coleman School had made its first flyer—Irvin E. Wells had soloed and had the makings of a very good pilot. Marie Dickerson was about ready to solo. Wesley Cotton only had about two hours to go before he would be turned loose.

But Neely was frantic—the Executive Group could not be filled. He could not raise the necessary amount of capital to incorporate. It seemed next to impossible to raise any money in Los Angeles among Negroes. Several Jews, having heard of the proposition, wanted to finance it. But that is just what Neely was trying to avoid. He wanted the control in the hands of Negroes.

So now Bill pressed his idea of getting the Executive Group from various other cities. At the next meeting of the incorporators it was decided to purchase a new Ford car and to appropriate expenses for Neely to journey to the different cities to put the proposition up to our various leaders. Ed. Graham was to go along as chauffeur; so the car was purchased, and Neely and Graham made ready to depart. The purchase of the car and the expense money for Neely and Graham did not leave enough money even to carry on the training, but Neely said he would raise money as soon as he left Los Angeles. In the meantime, the Operations Group decided to start a series of short hops in the American Eagle for the purpose of giving its members cross country flying and navigation training, as well as to advertise the company.

So early one morning, Bill, Banning, and Marie Dickerson took off from Lincoln Airport and headed the Eagle toward San Diego. The purpose of this trip was to familiarize Marie with the use of the compass and drift indicator. Ordinarily, flyers usually fly this trip without the use of either compass or drift indicator, since the course lies along the coast line and is very easy to follow, except when it is foggy—and that occurs very frequently. It was very clear that morning, but for the purpose of instruction Marie was instructed to lay off the course. Examination of the air map showed that Los Angeles to San Diego should be plotted in two courses, i. e. Los Angeles to Oceanside, eighty-four miles, and Oceanside to San Diego, thirty-four miles. This is necessary to keep from flying out too far over the ocean.

The first leg of the trip showed a true course of 132 degrees. Weather reports showed the wind at Los Angeles Harbor to be 270 degrees at twenty miles per hour velocity. The air speed indicator registered ninety miles per hour, showing that the OX was really turning up at its best. Plotting these two vectors, Marie found the resulting vector, or the corrected true course to be 141 degrees. This triangle also showed a ground speed of 104 m.p.h. Marie was quite surprised at this figure, stating that she did not know that the OX5 motor could carry the Eagle that fast. Bill then explained to her that any plane having a wind on its tail would travel along faster in proportion to the speed of the wind, and this west wind was almost a tail wind. At any rate it helped them along considerably. Having corrected the course for wind drift, it then became necessary to get the corrected magnetic course. Since the variation at Los Angeles was 16 degrees East, and at San Diego 15 degrees East, they decided to use the average variation of 15 degrees, 30 minutes. Applying this variation and using the familiar rule, "Variation East, Magnetic Least", the corrected magnetic course was found to be 125 degrees, 30 minutes. The deviation card for that heading showed a deviation of 3 degrees West. Again applying the rule "Deviation West, Compass Best", the corrected compass course was found to be 128 degrees, 30 minutes. Hence this was the course to steer to reach Oceanside. The ship had a compass in both the front and rear cockpit. Bill was in the front cockpit with Marie, and Banning was flying the ship. Bill told Marie that she was the Navigator and had to tell Banning which way to go. She had never been on a long flight before, and hence Bill was quite amused when Marie pulled the throttle and told Banning to follow a compass course of 128 degrees, 30 minutes.

Banning, who knew every inch of the route from Los Angeles to San Diego, left the course to get a glimpse of the warships anchored in San Pedro Harbor, quite forgetting Marie and her navigation, but Marie set up such a howl that he soon pulled back on the course. Bill then asked Marie how long they would be getting to Oceanside. A slight hesitation and Marie wrote down the following formula on an envelope that she had in her hand:

$$t = \frac{d}{s} = \frac{84}{100} \times 60 = 48 \text{ minutes}$$

"Forty-eight minutes", she replied. Bill was elated at the rapidity with which she figured, and felt that some day she might make a real navigation teacher.

Although they ascertained the wind direction from the weather report, Marie took a couple of readings with the drift indicator to check up on the report, and found out that Colonel Hersey, the "weather man", really knew his stuff, as the drift angle showed 9 degrees each time.

When they reached Oceanside, Marie was certainly surprised when Bill reminded her to look at the time, which showed that they had been flying 48½ minutes exactly. This gave her great confidence in her instruments, and her instruction and the methods used.

The trip was delightful, since the air was smooth and very fresh off the ocean, and, after flying over Long Beach, the entire journey lay about half a mile out over the ocean. The foaming white waves lashing against the coast formed quite a contrast to the blue ocean and the blue sky overhead; from an altitude of two thousand feet this made quite a picture. Bill wouldn't let Marie plot the last leg of the course before starting, as he wanted her to get the experience of plotting a course in the air. So, a little before reaching Oceanside, she began calmly plotting the new heading: True course 164 degrees.

This time Bill would not let her use the weather report to get the wind direction and velocity. He told her she must get the wind direction from the drift indicator, and that she must act as though she had no weather report. So she set to work accordingly. The drift indicator showed a drift angle of 9 degrees. Hence the corrected true course was found to be 173 degrees. Applying the variation she found the corrected magnetic course to be 157 degrees 30 minutes, and, the deviation being 2 degrees East, the course to steer was computed as 155 degrees 30 minutes. So Marie wrote on a piece of paper and passed it back to Banning: "Course to steer, 155 degrees 30 minutes." Banning nodded and smiled, as he swung the nose around farther to the south just as he was passing over the emergency landing field at Oceanside.

Presently the thousands of white buildings at San Diego hove in sight. Marie's navigation was perfect and, it being clear, she could check up on herself and see just exactly how far off she was. This gave her much confidence in her method. Approaching Ryan Airport, Banning pulled the nose of the ship up into a steep wing over, as was his custom upon approaching a new field for a landing, then glided in for a perfect three-point landing right on the circle. He taxied up to the hangar. They seemed to be a curiosity. All eyes were turned upon them. Never before had a Negro landed a plane on Ryan Airport. There was one colored fellow at the field watching the planes land. He was quite surprised, though elated, to see all Negroes get out of the plane. He walked over and introduced himself as Melvin White. He said that he had been interested in flying for quite some time but did not have the opportunity to learn. Bill told him that they had a Miss Corona White of Los Angeles in the organization.

"Corona? She's my sister", exclaimed Melvin joyfully.

"Then, I guess you and I are cousins", said Bill.

After quite a chat, Melvin drove the flyers to town to the Douglass Hotel, where he treated them to dinner. After sampling San Diego's chicken output they visited Tate's Funeral Home and Craft's Realty Parlors.

They remained a little too long on these visits, and were a trifle late for the return trip, as it was quite late in the afternoon when White drove them back to the airport.

After warming up the motor, they noticed that they had only little over an hour to get back to Los Angeles before sunset. The fog was rising slowly too. Banning opened the throttle, and in a jiffy they were passing over La Jolla on their way home. Marie figured her course as usual. And good that she did. She was now about to experience some of the reasons why navigation is necessary. The fog began to rise fast. It was blowing in from ahead. There was a head wind. However, Banning could see the top of the fog which appeared to be about 4,500 feet. So he started climbing. Soon he was on top, and to their great surprise there was a dense carpet of clouds between them and the ground—or ocean, whichever it was they were flying over—they could see neither.

However, a more beautiful sight could not have been found. The sun was just setting in the golden West, and its rays cast upon the clouds below caused them to glisten with myriads of bright colors. The sky above was blue, and the ground could not be seen at all. Marie looked somewhat disturbed. She was trying in vain to see the ground below, but not a hole was in sight in the clouds. Luckily the course was all plotted, and they had an accurate compass, for they would not have known whether they were flying out ten or twelve miles over the ocean, or whether they were headed inland toward the mountains. So the first leg of the hop they flew twenty minutes, which, according to computations, would put them over Oceanside. Then they changed their course, flying the last leg in fifty-five minutes. Those fifty-five minutes seemed like five hours, for each one realized that if they deviated just a trifle from their course they could be carried far out over the ocean, or over the mountains in the other direction. All eyes stayed fixed on the compasses. Banning noticed the grave faces and suddenly pulled the throttle, the motor revving down as though something was wrong. Bill, however, noticed the throttle in the front cockpit, and looked back at Banning and smiled, realizing that he was pulling one of his jokes. Marie, on the other hand, felt quite distressed. Bill's mind drifted to the beauty of the clouds below him. "If only everyone could have the opportunity to see such a sight," thought he, "then everybody would fly."

With only five minutes to spare, Banning started looking for a hole in the clouds to come through. Everyone joined in the search, but no holes were in sight. After straining their eyes for several minutes and flying in a circle, Marie suddenly spied a small hole, and like a flash Banning was doing a tight spiral through this hole. At times the fog completely enveloped them, leaving them flying blind for a few seconds; these seconds seemed like minutes. What a change! On top it was nice and light, the sun having just set, while under the fog it was nearly dark, and there were no navigation lights on the plane. That meant that they had to land immediately. But a strange thing happened just at the moment they came through the fog. The motor quit as though water had got into the carburetor, and Banning had to do some fast thinking. Making a 180 degree turn into the wind, he landed in an orange grove, knocking down two small orange trees just set out. Other than paying $25 for the damage to the two trees, they were none the worse off for their experience.

At Start of Trip

Neely and Graham were now all set to take off on their tour in the Ford car. Neely had much confidence that he could interest some "big shots" in the proposition. So with Ed Graham at the wheel as chauffeur, Neely assumed the role of advance agent.

The first message from Neely was a card the next day from Phoenix, stating that the car, which was artistically designed with an aeroplane on each side, attracted much attention. The next message came

from San Antonio, Texas. Neely spent a few days trying to make connections with several "big shots" in that
city. Ed Graham cautioned Neely about spending so
much money entertaining these prospects at dinners
with no results—Neely only replied that a showing
was necessary in order to make the proper contact.
He was certain he would be successful in San Antonio,
as he wrote that on the morrow evening he was banqueting twenty men whom he had interested in the
proposition, each one of whom he had checked up on as
being worth $25,000 or more in actual cash.

Everything was going fine at the banquet. Speeches
were made praising the efforts of the Negroes in
aviation—many stating that the time was ripe for
them to enter this field, others praising members of
the Bessie Coleman organization for taking the initiative. Neely was just about to take out his pencil and
ask for the names of the highest bidders for the
vacant seats on the Executive Board, when one elderly
gentleman arose and asked Neely how could he as-
sure them that there were any Negro flyers at all,
or even any that had nerve enough to fly. He also
stated that he had read an article of recent date in
the newspapers that there were no Negro flyers holding licenses.

In vain Neely tried to explain to the group that he
had had that letter published, and that at that time one
of the flyers was on the inactive list but had since been
reinstated, and that several others were completing
courses now. This, however, did not satisfy the gentleman, who finally suggested that none of the San An-
tonians make any investments until the group of
Negro flyers would fly to San Antonio so they could
see them perform. This gentleman ended his speech
by saying that, personally, he did not believe there were
any Negroes with guts enough to fly. Finally all the
others present sided with this man, and nothing that
Neely or Graham could say or do would change their

minds. So the meeting broke up. Neely was a physical wreck and thoroughly disgusted.

"To think," said he to Graham, "they ate all that chicken and none of them pledged a single dime."

Then came a split between Neely and Graham, Graham contending that it was foolish to spend money dining and banqueting these prospects with no results, for soon the funds would be all gone.

Nevertheless, they moved on to Houston, Beaumont, Shreveport, and New Orleans, with the same results. About this time Neely's fund had vanished. He wired for more money. Bill sent him $200 additional. They moved on to Little Rock. A letter from Graham stated that the prospect of failure was affecting Neely terribly. He stated that he was not himself most of the time and that he was starting to drink.

This was a blow to Bill, who had never known Neely to drink to amount to anything, and he had always depended on him in a crisis. Neely tried again and again—Oklahoma City, Tulsa, Muskogee, then Kansas City.

At Kansas City, a letter from Graham reported that Neely was affected too greatly by his failure to produce, and that he had resorted to drink to such an extent that he was hurting the company, for the public noticed it.

A letter from a Prof. H. L. Washington of Kansas City corroborated Graham's statement; he further stated that with such a representative as Neely our wonderful organization was doomed. Nevertheless on to St. Louis they went. Graham suggested that they wire for Neely to return. A telegram to St. Louis just missed him, as he had moved on to Chicago. There Neely and Ed Graham came to blows. It was now necessary for Bill to act, and act quickly. So he wired Neely to return to Los Angeles immediately. Poor Neely—he was heart-broken, but set out for Los Angeles.

When they reached Oklahoma City on the return trip, Neely borrowed some money from a man he had known previously in Wichita, Kansas. The man gave him a check for $50, which Neely cashed in a drug store. But when the owner of the drug store went to the bank with the check there were no funds. Without warning the drug store owner had the car seized. Both Neely and Graham were quite chagrined and did not wish Bill to know the car had been attached, so they accepted a proposition of a young man in Oklahoma City, named Thomas Allen, to get the car released, providing they would let him in on the Operations Group as airplane mechanic. Allen paid $100 in releasing the car, and then fixed up the tires and did some minor mechanical work on the Ford, thus leaving the company indebted to him to the extent of about $200, according to his figures.

Neely and Graham then returned to Los Angeles. "When it rains, it pours."

The company plane was kept in the hangar at the Lincoln Airport. Every morning, William Browne would get the plane out of the hangar and drain the carburetor jets and warm up the motor. This was part of his routine mechanical training. He had a young friend, Sydney Walker, who accompanied him to the airport each morning. Walker wanted in the worst way to learn to fly. He was one of the kind who believe they can fly by reading about it in books. The morning after Neely returned, Browne, not being able to get out to the airport early, called his friend Sydney Walker, and asked him to get the plane out of the hangar and warm it up and have it ready for Marie, who was to do some solo flying that morning.

Walker came out about an hour earlier than usual and warmed the motor up. Having done this, with no one around, he decided to fly the ship a little bit, although he had never had any instructions. But he got into the ship just the same. One of the boys in another

hangar stated that the ship was seen to zigzag down
the field, suddenly rise straight up from the ground
about twenty-five feet, and then shoot straight down
like a bullet, crashing into the ground and catching
fire just after. Walker jumped out unscathed. What
were the boys to do? They carried no insurance
on the ship. Well, there was $3500 gone up in smoke,
the rest of the funds wasted on the advance trip,
and one of the members of the Operations Group ex-
pelled for negligence to duty—allowing some one else
to warm up the ship in his stead.

What were they to do? This was the time that they
should have stuck close together, but just the opposite happened. Those who were not in favor of the
advance trip, those who were not in favor of purchasing the plane when it was purchased, those who were
not in favor of giving the members of the Operations
Group their training free—all began an "I-told-you-
so," and the members of the Operations Group were
wondering and speculating as to what would be the
outcome since the plane was burned. Just at this time
Thomas Allen arrived from Oklahoma City to start as
mechanic for the group. He had told Neely and Graham that he was an airplane mechanic, but close questioning revealed that he was one of the many who
think they are airplane mechanics because they know
how to grind the valves. Allen went up for the mechanic's examination and failed terribly. What a predicament the group was in! And thus were added several more set-backs for Bill in his quest to win the
bet from Rev. Braddan.

All these reversals did not deter Bill, however. He
called a meeting of the incorporators and asked for
suggestions as to what should be done. But there were
no ideas forthcoming. Neely had no new ideas. The
meeting adjourned until the morrow night to give each
one time to think.

The next morning there came a letter from the

president of the Mississippi State Fair Association stating that if the Bessie Coleman Clubs would bring an airplane to their State Fair for exhibition purposes during the week of the Fair, they would guarantee the club $2500.

So, at the meeting that night, spurred on by this offer, Neely had one more suggestion. "We'll get a ship and be there. Bill, you and Banning will fly there, and I will drive there with some one else of the group, and we will make the necessary contacts to put the proposition over."

But how were they to get a ship? All the money was gone and none was forthcoming. Even Bill, who came to Los Angeles with $7,000, had spent down to his last $1,000. But he came forth and said he would put in the thousand as he was in aviation to stay.

So, armed with the proposition of the State Fair and Bill's $1,000, Neely set out again with bright hopes to "proposition" a plane.

Neely worked fast, for in a couple of days he had paid down $1,000 on a wonderful little airplane, a Kinner Crown, and he and Bill had signed a ninety day note for the balance of $4,000. But the next day the vice president of the Crown Motor Carriage Co. said his company wished to help them all right, but that investigation showed that the company was just a new one and had no rating, and that they must ask for additional security. Neely drooped again, but Mrs. Hancock said she would put up one of her rent houses for additional collateral. Everybody was happy again. The club now had another airplane, and it was a beauty— air-cooled motor, booster magneto for starting, navigation lights, and brakes. So everything was made ready for the trip to Jackson. All that was necessary now was the money for gasoline and oil for the car and airplane, and expense money.

For publicity purposes, Banning and Bill posed in front of the ship for pictures. A cut was made of this picture for advertising in Negro newspapers. But a heated argument, over the cost of mats pursuant to Oliver Betts' contract, finally resulted in Bill's tearing up the contract, and Betts left the organization in a very hostile frame of mind. This hostility was later manifested by adverse publicity which it was very difficult for Bill and the organization to overcome.

More trouble loomed up. Every one in the group wanted to go to Jackson, but Banning, the chief pilot, decided that only two should go in the plane, as he didn't want to load it down going over the mountains. This meant that Bill would go as navigator and Banning as pilot. However, Allen, newly arrived from Oklahoma City, insisted that he should go as mechanic. He then proceeded to tell everyone he contacted about town that, had it not been for him, Neely could not have got back, and that the organization would have lost the car.

Bill suggested that Allen drive Neely in the car, instead of Graham. Then Allen calmed down. So Neely got busy trying to raise funds for the trip. Time grew short. No funds were raised. They could only scrape up enough expense money for the airplane. Two more days passed. It was now too late for the car to make the trip. Allen, incensed because he would not get to Jackson, tried to get the incorporators to call off the flight entirely. He said that, as badly as things were progressing here, if Bill and Banning got away they would never return.

However, the day of the take-off came. While Banning was warming up the motor, Neely called Bill aside.

"Well, so long, old Pal. I wish you much success in your aeronautical career", said Neely, extending his hand to Bill.

This puzzled Bill. "Why such a statement at this time, Neely?"

"Well, Pal, I'm through", said Neely.

"Through with what?" asked Bill, frantically.

"Bill, I have been a complete failure, a disgrace to the company, and the movement is too great for anyone, even me, to stand in its way. I'll never get over what I did just at the time I should have been strongest. The members of the company no longer have respect for me. I have lost the company but I have gained this—I'll never drink again. The time and money I have put into the company I hope will bear fruit. I hope it will be beneficial to someone of my race some day. Good luck, and carry on."

And before Bill could get over the shock and say anything, Neely jumped into the car with Allen and they drove away, and the last Bill heard of Neely he was somewhere in Arizona, prospecting for gold. There was a man with great ambitions, wonderful ideas, a willing worker, a hard worker—a man who, although not interested in flying himself, contributed much to the advancement of Negro progress in aviation, though few know it; and some day after the organization attains the success which is due it, it would be a wonderful thing to reinstate and reimburse Neely for his time and money, and for the splendid ideas he advanced to awaken the Negro from his slumber to enter into this great field of industry—aviation.

And so Bill suffered his greatest set-back in his effort to win his bet with Rev. Braddan.

CHAPTER VII

They were on the field ready to go at seven o'clock that morning, but Neely's resignation had knocked all the "go" out of them. Notwithstanding the fact that the motor was all warmed up, when Neely said he was quitting, Bill told Banning to "cut the switch," and started in search of Neely. Four hours of search brought no trace of him. No one had seen him. So at three o'clock the motor was again revved up for the take-off. Starting so late in the afternoon, the boys decided to fly to San Diego, stop over for the night, and take off at daybreak the next morning.

The plane they were flying was new to both of them, they having put in only two hours each on the job. Everything now in readiness, they taxied up to the end of the long concrete runway of the Grand Central Air Terminal for the take-off, flying dual, that is, with the controls in both cockpits connected so that either pilot might fly the ship at will.

Getting the white flag from the man in the tower as a signal to start, Banning "gave 'er the gun" and the little ship roared down the runway and soon was in the air. The little Crown left the ground long before it was expected to, and its rate of climb was quite surprising—better by far than any other similar plane in the 100-horse power type. This at least raised the boys' spirits, which were very low. One wide circle over the airport to gain altitude, and then the nose of the Crown was pointing toward Long Beach. Waving a farewell to those assembled at the airport beneath, they soon left Glendale in the distance. Both knew the route to San Diego so well that it was not necessary even to refer to maps or compass. Heading the ship equidistant between the white tower of the Los Angeles City Hall and the brown mosque-like building known as the Shrine Auditorium, two very good landmarks, they soon sighted Long Beach airport. Then, swinging the nose a bit to the left, they soon were following the coast line to San Diego.

Just as they approached San Clemente a startling thing happened. There was a layer of clouds about 3,000 feet up. They were flying under this cloud at about 2,000 feet. As the Crown approached a patch of clouds considerably lower than the rest, the roar of an airplane motor, quite near, was heard above the noise of the Kinner motor, which was cruising along nicely, and before the boys had a chance even to look about them a large white biplane in a power dive flashed out of the cloud just 100 feet in front of the Crown. A cold chill ran up Bill's spinal column, for had they been one second faster there would have been a terrible crash in mid-air. He watched the plane continue its dive fully another thousand feet before it levelled out. The pilot must have been flying above the clouds, and reaching his destination, probably decided to dive through the clouds.

Shortly afterwards they landed at the Ryan Airport, San Diego, and put the ship in the hangar for the night. They called Melvin White on the 'phone, and he came to the airport and drove them to the hotel. After eating dinner, and being away from the turmoil of Los Angeles, their minds began to function properly. They then realized that they had left without a canteen of water, sandwiches, etc., but felt that with such a good performing airplane they would have no trouble in reaching their destination, so didn't bother further. They did purchase two pint cans of tomatoes, which could be used to quench one's thirst in an emergency.

About 9 o'clock that night in the hotel, Bill lay

down on the bed, and opened his brief-case to plot the course for the following day. To his great surprise they had left Los Angeles without bringing maps, protractor, dividers, or any navigating instruments. Bill immediately put his shirt and shoes back on, and went into the streets to find a protractor and some air maps. He searched all over the downtown section, but it was too late. The stores in San Diego close early. The only map he found was a Rand McNally road map which he purchased at a filling station. They only had three days left to get to Jackson, Miss., so they decided to push off at daybreak and take a chance on getting maps at Phoenix. They felt they could estimate the course to Phoenix from the road map.

Next morning at 4:30, Melvin White knocked at the door of their room. He had an auto waiting outside to take the boys to the airport. Having dressed, they stopped at the only restaurant open that time of the morning in that vicinity—a Greek restaurant, which was not as clean as it could have been, and so neither of the boys would eat anything, just ordered a cup of coffee, saying they would eat when they reached El Centro.

At 5:15 they arrived at the airport. Assisted by the attendant, the ship was placed on the line. They had difficulty in starting the motor that morning, notwithstanding the fact that the ship was equipped with a booster magneto. The carburetor jets were drained, but not a sign of life from the motor. Finally, after all three had exhausted themselves pulling the propeller through, the motor started. After warming up for about eight minutes, the temperature gauge and oil pressure gauge showed that everything was O.K. for the start. Melvin gave them a hearty handshake and bade them good luck as Banning opened the throttle, and the Crown was once more in the air. Bill noticed that Banning was developing a lot of confidence in the Crown, for instead of climbing to about 4,000 feet before heading for the mountains, he straightened out at 2,000 feet, pointing the nose straight down Broadway in San Diego, which course would lead them straight over El Centro. This made the Crown have to show a pretty high rate of climb in order to clear the 7,000 foot range looming up so closely ahead. But she made it with much to spare. Wonderful little ship! So elated was Banning, that, while over the highest range, he closed the throttle and yelled to Bill that this was some ship, to which Bill nodded his approval. Just then the air speed indicator quit functioning. This caused no great alarm at this time.

The wonderful performance of the ship, however, caused the boys to get into trouble. Banning let the plane climb, for no other reason than to see how far up it would go, and at 10,000 feet up the small towns were not so discernible. This was the highest either of the boys had been up, and they didn't realize that the altitude greatly affected their seeing their landmarks. The objective was El Centro, which was south of the Salton Sea. Having passed over the mountains they started looking for the Salton Sea, hoping to locate El Centro from it. Banning looked about, closed the throttle, and said they were 'way off the course. He said he saw the Salton Sea 'way to his right, when as a matter of fact it should be on their left. He pointed out to Bill the sea of water south of them. But Bill argued that it didn't seem possible that they could be that far off, for he was sure they had been travelling almost directly due East True, which at that time should put them directly over El Centro.

So Banning cocked the ship up into a steep right bank and headed for the body of water he had just pointed out. Bill closed the throttle and said he knew it was not possible for them to be so far off the course. But Banning was chief pilot, and so they headed on in the new direction. Presently they reached this sea of water, and Banning continued on to the south, against the protests of Bill, who thought they were going wrong. But he was not certain either, for this body of water certainly was the shape of the Salton Sea, and, if it was the Salton Sea, then Banning was right, for El Centro lay south of it.

Having flown about one-half hour south of this body of water, Bill said they should be over El Centro. So they began to descend. As they descended closer to the mountains, wind currents set up by the ranges caused the air to get terribly rough. The front cockpit of the Crown was very spacious. Bill had his handbag beside him in the front seat. The strap was buckled over Bill's waist and then over one end of the handbag. While looking about trying to locate where they were, the handbag slipped from under the strap, and was just resting on the seat. Suddenly, passing from one mountain ridge to another, the boys encountered the worst "bump" they have ever experienced. The ship actually dropped about 300 feet. When this happened, and before Bill could gain his poise, he looked up, and there was the handbag about 12 feet up in the air. Luckily it fell within reaching distance of Bill, who grabbed it and jerked it back into the seat. The same thing might have happened to Bill had he not been strapped to the plane. But the strap was loose, and Bill experienced a funny feeling of having the plane drop out from under him, as though he were suspended in the air for a second, when the pressure of the strap finally pulled him down with the plane. All this while Banning was fighting the controls of the plane, which was being tossed about like a piece of paper in a storm.

They descended to 3,500 feet. The terrain was plainly visible now, but it was all mountainous. They could not be near El Centro, because El Centro is in a valley—the Imperial Valley. In fact, they should now be able to see several little towns in the vicinity of El Centro, but not a telegraph post, not a railroad, not a house, not a dog, cat or chicken could be seen. Where could they be? They had now been flying two and one-half hours and only had forty-five more minutes of gasoline. Which way should they turn? A distressed look came over Banning's face. Forty-five minutes flying would not carry them back to the last civilization they had seen. Just then, Banning touched Bill on the head and pointed ahead. Bill looked, but saw nothing. Banning closed the throttle and yelled, "The desert. El Centro is just beyond that desert."

Bill looked again. He did see a vast expanse of something that looked like sand. So onward they went toward this seeming desert. Still straining his eyes ahead, Bill suddenly closed the throttle and said, "That's not a desert, that's water. It looks like the ocean."

Banning replied that Bill was seeing things, but ten minutes more flying convinced him that they were approaching a large body of water.

"We'd better land here and get our bearings," said Bill. But on descending to 500 feet they could see that the ground was covered with cactus and large rocks which prevented their landing. So on they headed toward the water. Presently the motor coughed. They were out of gas. They were forced now to make a landing, which Banning did on a nice sandy beach on the water's edge.

Where were they? What body of water was this? They did not know. However, they were glad to have made a safe landing. They were in a terrible plight. Gasoline gone, and only two days to get to the Jackson Fair. Taking out the automobile map, they began trying to locate themselves.

"We must be in Mexico," said Bill.

"Yes," said Banning. "This large body of water can only be the Pacific Ocean. But how far south of the border can we be?"

"We can't be very far south," said Bill. "If we

walk north along the beach we will certainly run into Ensenada very soon."

It was 10 A.M. when they decided to tie the ship down and head north, when Banning suddenly exclaimed, "Look here. I see now why we went wrong." Bill rushed to the rear cockpit where Banning was standing. "See, the compass is haywire. The nose of the ship is pointed into the ocean, but yet the compass shows that the ship is headed East."

"Yes, that's it," said Bill. "The compass certainly shows East. I wonder how long it has been off?"

With these words the boys started up the beach in the direction they thought was North, with nothing but the two cans of tomatoes and the road map. They figured they would soon reach a little town and get gasoline, then get their bearings, and be off to Jackson. But fate had decreed otherwise. They had walked about four hours, and had ran into no signs of civilization whatsoever. They were quite thirsty—the water along which they walked was salt water.

Suddenly Bill stopped. "What's the matter?" asked Banning.

Bill said nothing. He plucked a twig from a sage brush and stuck it in the ground. It cast a shadow. Bill made a mark on the ground where the shadow was cast. In about three minutes he made another mark on the ground, and sank down in disgust, without saying a word.

"What is the matter with you?" Banning asked again.

"Well, listen to the sad news," Bill commenced. "We have been travelling south instead of north these four hours. And the compass is not haywire. It is all right, and this is not the Pacific Ocean."

Banning burst out in a fit of laughter. Nothing was more absurd, he thought. "Well, I suppose it's the Atlantic Ocean," he said, laughing heartily.

But his laughter soon turned almost to tears as Bill

explained: "You see, I made the marks on the ground to determine definitely the direction the sun was moving. The shadow cast indicates that the sun is moving away from this body of water that we suppose to be the Pacific Ocean. As a matter of fact, if this is really the Pacific Ocean, then the sun should set behind or in the ocean. You know, Banning, *the sun never fails* to set in the West. Well, the sun is moving away from the water. We know definitely that the Pacific Ocean is West and we know that the sun sets in the West, so this then can not be the Pacific Ocean."

"Well, I'll be damned. You know I couldn't get it into my head that we had circled all the way back to the Pacific Ocean; so the instrument is right after all. Well, I guess when we learn to depend entirely upon accurate instruments, we will be a lot better off, for man's judgment is sometimes so wrong."

They then turned about, regretting that they had to retrace their steps. At 6 P.M. they reached the ship. Eight hours walk for nothing. They were tired out, hungry, and thirsty. They started to open one of the cans of tomatoes, but counselled against it, as they had no idea where they were. Bill figured out that the only place they could be was on the Bay of Lower California, on the eastern coast of Baja California, Mexico. It was possible that they were three hundred miles south of the border. In that case the question was whether there were any Mexican towns or villages along this coast, and, if not, could they hold out without food or water until they reached civilization. They had no map of Mexico, so they had no idea how far they had to travel.

Not knowing whether the country was infested with wild animals or not, they decided to sleep in the cockpit of the ship that night, and start out at daybreak next morning. Probably they would run into someone in time to get out and at least get to Jackson before the Fair was over.

So, as the sun ceased to warm the earth with its rays, the cool breezes ushering in the shades of night-fall caused a cold shudder to fall upon our two colored aces, leaving two shivering forms breathing hard in an effort to snatch a few hours rest 'way out on a bleak desert, seemingly miles and miles from any human being, with only the dreary roar of the ocean waves lashing against the shore, and the occasional rustling of the sage brush to break the silence of the black darkness.

It was a long time before Bill could go to sleep, but just before dozing off, he recalled that at night, lights are visible for a great distance, and so he stood up on top of the fuselage of the plane to get an elevated view of the surrounding country, hoping to see the lights of a village or of an automobile passing in the distance. But, alas, no such good luck—there were lights to be seen, but only those bright lights thrown out by Mars, Venus, Jupiter, and thousands of other stars high up in the firmament, telling the boys that, although they had no shelter for the night and no blankets with which to cover their heads, there would be no rain or dew to disturb their slumber.

CHAPTER VIII

LAS LUCES DE SAN FELIPE

The night was cold—quite a contrast to the heat of the previous day, but typical of the desert climate of Mexico; so when daybreak came, no alarm clock was necessary to awaken the boys, for they were already restlessly looking forward to the dawn of the day, hoping the sun would soon come to lend them its heat.

Again they took a long look at the little Crown tied down amidst the sagebrush and mesquite, as they started down the beach to—they didn't know where—but this time in an opposite direction from that in which they started the day before.

As it grew lighter they saw many shells strewn along the beach, and hence concluded that there must be oysters about; so, down to the water's edge they went in search of breakfast, but all the shells turned out to be empty. They wondered what had happened to all the insides, why so many empty shells while they could not find a single one with an oyster in it. But soon this riddle was solved, for many sea gulls were seen to dive into the water, and each bird rose up with an oyster in its beak. Before getting far, it had pried open the shell, swallowed the contents, and dropped the shell into the bay to be eventually washed ashore. It was amazing how those sea gulls could use their beaks.

Walking along the beach now was quite pleasant, especially as the sun was just beginning to rise, and the cool, fresh salt air was exhilarating to the lungs, and the boys breathed deeply of it. How wonderful they would have felt had they only had a good breakfast of ham and eggs and toast! They now recalled that they did not eat anything the previous morning at the Greek restaurant, which they now regretted. For about two hours the beach was level sand, and walking was just good exercise, but soon they reached a rocky coast. Then they had to leave the beach and walk inland through the desert sand, where walking became work, for they slid back a half step for every step forward they took, so that when the sun was high in the heavens perspiration began to pop out and trickle down their backs. Bill had gone his limit with his can of tomatoes. He just had to open it, and did so just as the rock-strewn coast again dissolved into a sandy beach, visible as far as the eye could see. They sat down in the sand, and, not having a knife, resorted to a rock and a key to make a hole in the can. My! how delicious! It was the first drink or bite to eat they had since the cup of coffee at the Greek restaurant. Finally the can was emptied. What a relief! Suddenly Bill grasped Banning's arm, and pointing to two row boats 'way out in the bay exclaimed, "We're saved at last."

They waved, they whistled—they took off their white coveralls and waved, but not being able to attract any attention, they sat down to wait until the boats came in. They thought they were fishing and surely would come in soon. Later on they began to shout and wave again. But no reply. They waited about an hour and a half, when suddenly up in the air went two large pelicans. These were what the boys had thought were row boats, and to think they lost an hour and a half shouting to those giant pelicans that stood much higher than men!

Again with spirits depressed, and more so because they had wasted so much time, they trudged along in the hot sun for about three hours; then exhausted, both fell down in the sand and in a jiffy were fast asleep. About an hour's rest and they were again on their way. They now began to pick up speed, since the sun's rays were much cooler, due to the fact that soon it would hide itself beyond the western hills. The fact that they had not eaten for two days now began to tell on them—they were getting weak.

The shades of night soon came, but on they marched into the darkness. The night air invigorated Bill and he felt stronger, but Banning wanted rest; he was weakening. They stopped awhile. Banning slept like a log, but the darkness of the night and the illusions of various forms creeping about kept Bill wide awake. After about an hour's rest, Bill roused Banning and they were off again. Suddenly, about the same time, they both seemed to be aware of the fact that something was following them. Glancing back over their shoulders, they could see the form of some animal that stopped when they stopped and continued when they did—and they didn't even have a pocket knife with them, neither was there a stick to be found, as shrubbery was very scarce. Only occasionally they ran across sagebrush and mesquite. The creature following them caused them some discomfort. They could not run, they were too weak; but he did cause them to cover much more territory, and they did not stop again for rest. Once more Bill thought about the lights. They approached a small hill. Bill climbed to the top to see if he could see any lights in the distance, but none were in sight.

About one o'clock Banning said he would just as soon be eaten alive by a wild animal as to die from exhaustion and lack of rest, so in spite of the animal following, he stopped and dropped to the ground, fast asleep. Bill's mind rested on the animal, which stopped too. Banning had a little box of matches, so Bill hustled up a little sagebrush and made a fire. He recalled that animals are afraid of fire, so he began to make a large circle around Banning and lighted it. Soon he, too, had fallen asleep, awakening only at intervals to place more sagebrush and greasewood on the fire, or to turn the other side of his body, which had got cold, to the fire. At daybreak the following morning, Banning aroused himself and then woke Bill. The animal was gone. They made their regular trip to the water's edge in search of oysters, and finding none, only washed their faces. They tried to drink a little of the salt water, but it nauseated them even to rinse their mouths out with it, it was so salty.

The Fair at Jackson had started by this time, so the boys' only hope now was to get back to civilization alive. All the while, Banning, full of his jokes, would ask Bill how would he enjoy a good hot bowl of Cream of Wheat, or the back of a fried chicken—this only making Bill feel worse. Seeing another large stretch of empty shells they went down to the water's edge to search for oysters again, but found none. They saw plenty of fish jumping up out of the water, especially barracuda, but they had neither hook nor line, and certainly no bait. While looking about, though, Bill noticed a snail on a rock. He recalled having eaten snails in France. Yes, they are considered a delicacy over there, he explained to Banning. Only these snails were much smaller than the French snails Bill had eaten. Nevertheless they collected a couple of dozen. They then opened the last can of tomatoes and drank the contents. This invigorated them greatly. Leaving about one-fourth of the tomato juice in the can they put the snails into it, and made a fire and cooked them. After a while, Bill pronounced the snails done.

But what a terrible taste! They did not taste like the French snails, Bill averred, but it was at least something in their stomachs, and really strengthened them; although they learned later that these snails are not the edible kind. Bill then said that if they found nothing else, they might keep alive on snails, and so they carried their tomato can along with them. But, alas, they never were able to find another snail.

It seemed as though the third day was hotter, and

the higher the sun got in the sky, the weaker Bill got. Bill had to stop and rest, but Banning was active and fresh. Strange, it seemed that during the day, Bill was weak and inactive, while Banning was O.K., but during the night Banning was all in and Bill was fresh.

Late that afternoon, they noticed the bones of prehistoric animals, hardened like stone. They actually saw the spinal column of an animal every bit forty feet long and a pelvic bone that was fifteen feet across the largest part. While examining these bones they noticed several bushes of red berries. They were quite sweet and delicious, but they decided not to eat any as Bill said they looked like the berries he used to see when he was a boy in Kentucky, and his mother told him they were poison berries. So they decided not to eat any of them, because they would rather die of exhaustion than be poisoned 'way out there, and Banning added that he hoped his death would come in an airplane. These berries were growing all along the route that they followed for the next two days.

Night came on. As usual, Bill mounted the nearest hill to look for lights. Suddenly he called Banning, who very reluctantly and with difficulty mounted to the top of the hill.

"Look," said Bill. "See those lights, they must be the lights of a town."

"Ah, you're seeing stars again", said Banning, disgusted after climbing the hill.

And so Bill finally left the hill, after assuring himself that they were stars. That night as usual Banning was all in, and Bill gathered the sagebrush and made the fire. They aroused themselves the fourth morning at daybreak, weak, weary, hungry, thirsty, but determined to carry on. Along about noon both the boys had walked out of their shoes entirely. They were barefooted. Their tongues began to swell and their lips to parch.

Walking along the water's edge, Banning saw a

large fish swimming very close to the shore in the shallow water. He had his leather jacket on his arm. Suddenly he dived into the water, with the coat, after the fish. But the fish got away and Banning got soaking wet. But he made a discovery. Falling into the water was almost the same as taking a good drink of water. So they immediately pulled off their clothes and went in bathing. What a discovery! How refreshing! It seemed as though every pore in their bodies opened to take in a drink. They were refreshed beyond words. And so we find them stripping down every three or four hours to take a drink, as they called it.

Other than the worn out shoes, the frequent baths, fruitless searches for oysters and snails, passing up the berries, thinking they were poison, the fourth day passed as usual, except that they were getting weaker and weaker.

The sun was high in the sky when they awoke on the fifth morning. Banning declared that to be a good omen, as they had always roused at daybreak. They were very weak by now and had lost much weight. They realized that if they did not reach civilization soon, or get something to eat and drink, the sea gulls would have more than oysters to feast on. They tried in vain to kill a sea gull with rocks.

Banning looked at Bill, his face was long, his beard long, his lips were parched, he had fallen off terribly. He wondered if he, too, looked as bad. "Do I look very bad, Bill?" asked Banning.

"No", said Bill. "Do I?"

"No", said Banning. But each realized that the other had never told a bigger lie. As the day grew hotter, Bill grew fainter. Rest periods were too frequent. They realized that they could not last another day and continue to walk, nevertheless they trudged on.

Bill slept nearly all that afternoon. In vain he tried to get Banning to go on, as he felt pretty good, but

Banning would not do so, so Bill would muster enough strength to continue. As night came on Banning played out completely. The cool air invigorated Bill. While Banning lay prostrate beside a fire that Bill made, Bill thought he would take a last look at the lights from yonder nearby hill. So he stole away and left Banning asleep. Climbing to the top of the hill about a quarter of a mile away, Bill thought he saw lights, but another look convinced him they were stars. Then, just as he turned to go back, he saw one of the lights go out. He pondered to himself. He had never heard of a star going out. Stars always shoot, thought he, and while he was thus thinking he saw the light come back on again. He was certain this was a light. His heart began to beat faster. He got stronger. He ran down the hill to where Banning was asleep. With some difficulty he woke Banning, who did not want to go up the hill, stating that Bill was still seeing stars. However, when Bill told him the light went out and then came on again he was interested, and, after some time, he succeeded in climbing to the top of the hill. While they looked at three lights together, a fourth light came on. Then, as if charged with a good chicken dinner and a couple of glasses of good Arrowhead water, the two men dashed down the hill in the direction of the lights. They followed the lights for several hours without rest, when suddenly Bill dropped exhausted. Banning fell down beside him, and soon both were fast asleep. About half an hour's rest and they were up again. The lights went out one by one, but they had the general direction and continued on.

At 2:00 A.M., they had not come to a village yet. They were getting alarmed again. Had they passed the place? They were sure there must have been a village or a few houses. Just then Bill could make out some huts in the distance, built of grass and mud. At the same time, dogs began to bark. Overjoyed, the boys pushed on toward the barking dogs. Presently they came right upon the huts, with the dogs barking terribly.

"Indians," said Banning, "and they say these Indians in Mexico are almost savage."

Before he could say any more a six-foot tall Indian stood towering over them. He called off the dogs but did not say a word. Being in Mexico Bill guessed that the official language was Spanish, and so he commenced as follows:

"Senor, tengo faim, tengo soif, ha sido cinco dias que han comidas. Pronto, agua."

THE VILLAGE

But the tall Indian said not a word. He only stared at them. Bill was just about to repeat his sentence of Spanish, thinking that he had not spoken distinctly, when a feminine voice from the inside of the hut said, "Pobre muchachos, pobre muchachos," and then said something to the Indian which Bill did not understand. The Indian grunted and rushed into the hut and came out with a pail of water and a gourd, which he shoved toward them. They both drank and drank, the best drink they had ever had. The woman in the hut told Bill in Spanish that she had nothing to eat in the house, but that the Indian would take them down to the

commissary and they could purchase what they wanted. Bill thanked her, and they moved on behind the big
Indian, who was taking such large strides that Banning fell out trying to keep up with him after drinking
so much water.

They paused about fifteen minutes before they
could go on. Presently, the Indian stopped at a rudely
constructed grocery, and, after much knocking and
shouting, a white man raised a long window. The Indian said something to him in his language. Bill then
told his story in broken Spanish, as best he could, and
the white man shoved out two large boxes of sardines,
two large bottles of "sodaria" as he called it, and two
boxes of crackers.

"Quantos?" Bill asked.

"Dos pesatas Mejicanas, un dollar American," he
replied.

"What did he say?" asked Banning.

But before Bill could answer Banning, the white
man broke in saying: "Hell, you are American! Why
didn't you say that, instead of trying to talk this crazy
language. I never did like it anyway. No charge. Now
tell me what happened, in English. I can understand
that and you can speak that." And so, after a long
talk, he gave them more food, and shelter for the night.

Just before retiring, Banning asked him what was
the name of this village.

He replied: "This is the fishing village of San
Felipe."

"Ah, said Bill, "then what I saw upon the hill were
"LAS LUCES DE SAN FELIPE" (The lights of San
Felipe).

CHAPTER IX

THE FIRST AIR SHOW

After two weeks of recuperation at San Felipe, eating frijoles (Mexican beans), fish, goose eggs, and tortillas, cooked by a beautiful Mexican senorita, the boys soon picked up a part of the weight they lost during their five days and nights trek through the desert without food or drink. It was strange, though, that, being exposed as they were, sleeping out in the open, on the damp sand, cold at night, hot during the day, wading through water, and with nothing to eat or drink, yet their health was wonderful.

San Felipe, a little fishing village of seventy-five people, was about 175 miles south of the Mexican border, to which the boys headed. They had travelled 135 miles during the five days and nights. This they checked with the aeroplane later on, it taking one hour and a half to fly the same distance. Hence the forced landing was 310 miles south of the Mexican border on the Gulf of Lower California.

They made three important discoveries while at San Felipe. They learned that there is a Mexican Salton Sea just south of the American Salton Sea. This Mexican lake is nearly the same shape and size as the American Salton Sea. It is called the Laguna Salada. It was this Laguna Salada that Banning saw when he thought he saw the Salton Sea. As a matter of fact the direction of the sun and the rays of the sun prevented his seeing the Salton Sea. At the time he saw the Laguna Salada the boys were right over El Centro, but were too high to recognize it. Consequently, mistaking the Laguna Salada for the Salton Sea, they travelled many miles south of their course and on into

the Mexican desert. They learned that they were not
the only pilots, however, to make this mistake.

They also learned that the coast along which they
travelled is noted for its fine oysters; they just didn't
know how to look for them. When they returned to
the airplane, many sack loads of oysters were loaded
from this same territory over which they had travelled

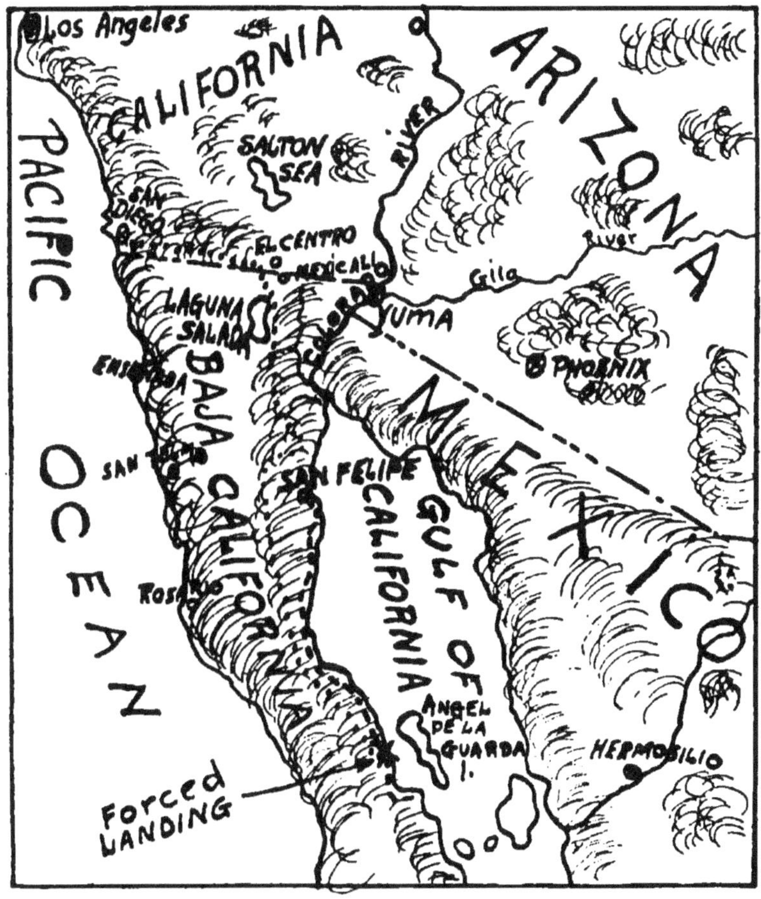

and nearly starved to death. One of the Mexican police
showed them that had they just thrust their hands
about four or five inches under the sand they would
have come across large beds of big, juicy, sweet oysters.
This they tried out and found it to be the truth. The

oysters were thick all along the coast. They also learned that the red berries they thought were poison were very palatable, and that the Mexicans relish them greatly.

They learned, too, that the area in which they landed is the area in which ships anchor that smuggle Chinese and dope into the United States. For that reason the Mexican Government sent police back to the plane with the boys to investigate, and this is why they were held incommunicado by the Mexican Government, pending an investigation in the United States as well.

BANNING AND THE MEXICAN POLICE

However, with the aid of the Mexican police, who were extremely cordial to the boys, gasoline was carried back to the ship, part way in a Ford car, part way in a motor boat, but the last twenty-five miles Banning and Bill had to carry the gasoline strung up in three five-gallon cans along a stick, which they supported upon their shoulders. They flew back to San Felipe and gave the girls in town and a few of the officials airplane rides, then headed for Yuma, at the mouth of the Colorado River.

At Yuma they were inspected by the United States Immigration Officials. After making several friends there, among them Mr. Woods, proprietor of the Woods' Hotel; Mr. Hulit, prominent business man; Miss Ursula Land, belle of the town, and Bob Hassell, an experienced automobile mechanic, who was interested in becoming an airplane mechanic, the boys headed toward Phoenix, Arizona.

At Phoenix, they sought to raise money to pay off the note on the airplane and return to Los Angeles. Through the wonderful cooperation of Mrs. Tomasita L. Lewis, Rev. Thomas Crain, and Dr. Robert Phillips, they were enabled to incorporate under the State Laws of Arizona with a permit to sell stock up to $10,000, including all the previous incorporators in Los Angeles, the three Phoenix people, and Melvin White of San Diego, who joined the boys in Phoenix just as soon as he heard they had returned.

With careful planning, a campaign was mapped out to start selling $10,000 worth of stock. Demonstrations were to be made with the airplane, and the boys hoped to raise enough immediately to pay off the note on the airplane. So a big demonstration was arranged for Phoenix. Several dollars were spent advertising this affair, which had attracted the attention of all the colored people of that city.

But while the boys were busy trying to carry on, someone else was busy in Los Angeles. Thomas Allen, who was disgruntled because he did not make the trip, got together with Oliver Betts and tried to stir up the Los Angeles incorporators by telling them that Bill and Banning had run away to raise money and would not return. Betts started a report that Bill had run away with thousands of dollars of the Los Angeles poor people's money, that he had influenced an old lady to sell her home to invest in the organization, and that she had lost the home. Allen succeeded in getting Mrs. Hancock to protect her collateral on the plane, and consequently, on the day of the big affair in Phoenix, when thousands of people began to assemble on the field, the sheriff came up to Bill and Banning and stated that he had papers to return the ship to Los Angeles. There was a Judge Smith on the field who told the sheriff that he did not think it necessary to attach the ship, that he felt assured the boys would fly the ship back to Los Angeles if told to do so. So the sheriff allowed them to go on with the demonstration. But a couple of fellows overheard the conversation of the sheriff and Judge Smith and spread the news through the crowd that the boys had stolen the airplane, and that the sheriff was there for it and to arrest the boys. And so, financially, the affair was disastrous. Several hundred people had come prepared to purchase stock after the demonstration, and it was certain about $5,000 could easily have been raised, had not this false report been spread about. To make things worse, the following week Betts' report received wide circulation in Negro newspapers throughout the country. This report killed the selling of any stock for the company forever. Just as Neely had said, it had so happened. It would now take some very effective and hard work ever to do any more good. But Bill was determined.

The first thing he did was to send Banning back to Los Angeles with the Crown airplane, in order that Mrs. Hancock's collateral could be released. In the meantime Mrs. Lewis and Dr. Phillips, who understood everything, planned day and night for a trip into Texas with another plane to raise money and carry through the proposition.

Banning flew the Crown back to Los Angeles, then returned to Phoenix. The day after he returned, while he and Bill were laying out plans, their door bell rang. Opening the door, two white men, who had the appearance of detectives, stepped in. They first asked the boys how they were progressing with their aeronautics. After learning that they were not doing so fine they flatly asked them if they wanted to make some real money. They then offered to pay $250 each for every Chinaman the boys would bring across the Mexican border. They said they would furnish each of the boys a seven-place cabin plane and all the gasoline and oil necessary. They claimed that it was so unusual to see colored fellows flying that no one would suspect them of carrying Chinamen or dope. They then left the boys to think it over, stating they would return sometime on the morrow.

JAMES HERMAN BANNING, CHIEF PILOT

"Well, what do you think of that, Bill?" said Banning as they left. "That's $1500 a load. Several loads of that and we could very easily put over the proposition."

"But if it ever became known, one's reputation would be ruined forever," said Bill.

"Whose reputation is ruined any worse than yours is now, after that write-up Betts gave you? Bill, you don't realize how many people throughout the country read that. It was featured in many colored papers. One of the Los Angeles papers carried headlines about it. If you made a few thousand dollars smuggling Chinamen, Betts would probably give you a wonderful write-up, but after spending $7,000 of your own money to advance aviation among Negroes, this is what you get. I don't know but that I will take up this offer."

"But, Banning, right will prevail. We can beat Betts, even if he does have influence with the press, and if I never do anything else, I will convince the public some day that Oliver Betts' report was false, and that he abused his influence to circulate it."

"But, Bill, we are broke, and these men will give us funds now. Think of that."

"Yes, that is true, but we must not do it. That is the last thing we must think about."

So on into the night the discussion went on, Banning finally deciding that he would not take up the men's proposition, but he swore he was going to look out for himself from then on.

So in a few days Banning and Bill prepared to start a barnstorming tour of Texas, accompanied by Mrs. Lewis and General Taylor, who was to drive Mrs. Lewis' big car. The airplane that they were to fly was an American Eagle, Kinner, and was owned by Mrs. Lewis, who was to take flying lessons en route.

The news soon spread all around Phoenix that Bill and Banning were about to embark on a barnstorming tour of Texas. The day before they left, while walking down Second Street, they were accosted by a group of fellows.

"Hey, cum here a minit, aviater," hollored the little stout colored fellow who was surrounded by a dozen or more friends engaged in a hot argument with him. "Can't you fellers land on any airport you want to?"

"Naw," replied the fellow with the grey suit whose hair was slicked back with so much Old Pal hair grease that his head looked like a mirror. "Naw, I'll answer for him. Naw, they can't. I've been all over the country and I know. In Kansas City they would not let

Dr. A. Porter Davis land his plane on the field, and I know if you can't land in Kansas City, you sho can't land in Texas."

"Aw, you're wrong. These fellers are licensed pilots, and they'll let 'em land anywhere," broke in the little fellow again.

"Well," said a lazy-looking chap, "they might have a license all right, but, bruther, take it from me, when they git to Texas, their license is counterfit."

So ran the argument in front of Ed Carter's pool hall when Bill and Banning passed by. And so much of this they heard on all hands that, on the 17th of June, when they were going to the airport to head for Texas, there was a slight fear in the boys' hearts that maybe they would have a little trouble.

Nevertheless, at 5:00 P.M. they reached the airport. Banning took the pilot's seat and Bill undertook the navigating. After warming up, Banning asked, "O.K.?" of Bill, who replied, "O.K." and soon the tail of the red American Eagle was in the air, and a few seconds later the ship rose from the ground, and headed across the east end of the Salt River Mountains south of Phoenix toward Tucson. About twenty miles out they passed Chandler, Arizona, and, while Bill passed away the time counting the number of streets in this little town, he experienced one of the blessings of flying in hot climates—the Eagle's nose was up, they were climbing, and the change in temperature was delightful and refreshing. Then Bill's sympathies ran with those less fortunate mortals in Phoenix and the little towns over which they were passing, sweltering under a tropical sun which ran the thermometer up to 110 degrees in the shade, while only fifteen minutes out of Phoenix they were enjoying a temperature of about 80 degrees, up in the air.

They are now passing over the Sacaton Mountains with the Piacho Reservoir in sight on the left. They head for the pass opposite Newman Peak. This is a good landmark for flyers over this route. The peculiar shape of the peaks on each side of the pass leaves an everlasting impression, and one remembers that after passing through this pass, Tucson looms up.

But it is getting bumpy. What's causing it? It is usually calm in this vicinity around 5:30 P.M. Oh, yes! Out to the left they notice two patches of clouds which seem to string from the heavens down to earth like two dull white misty veils, slowly moving in a direction which would take them right across the boys' path. They are two rainstorms which look as if they will run into the plane's course before the boys can pass them. But the old Kinner motor is given full throttle, and, just as they were abreast of the Tortolita Mountains, another drop in temperature greeted them, with a little moisture. Looking back a few seconds later, Bill saw they had just beaten the rainstorm across the path and the entire region behind them was enveloped in rain. The Tucson Mountains are now on their right, with Tucson at the foot of the mountains.

After circling over a certain house in town a couple of times, Banning headed for the Mayse Airport. Pretty lucky, this chap Banning—he doesn't like to walk; I don't know whether it is just because he doesn't like the exercise, or whether he has bad feet, but, anyhow, he always managed to make his circles over certain houses in certain towns in California and Arizona, and by the time he had landed at the airport, inspected the plane and put it in the hangar, some good looking young lady would drive up to the airport just in time to drive Banning to town. A new kind of radio—he should get a patent on it. The trip to Tucson, 110 miles, was made in one hour and ten minutes.

June 19th, they landed in El Paso, but Betts' false report had preceded them, and so the boys could do no good. They then journeyed to Abilene, Midland, Fort Worth, Dallas, Corsicana, Mejia, and everywhere they went they met the same thing. There was no use trying to continue with this situation existing. Banning was furious. So they decided to return to Los Angeles, but not until after visiting Jacksonville, Texas, which was Taylor's home. He had not been home for several years, and wanted the bunch to go there by all means so that the home folks could see that he was connected with a flying organization.

Accordingly, Taylor drove on ahead, as was the custom, to locate a landing field, for not all the small towns had airports. He wired back to Corsicana,

BARNSTORMING IN TEXAS

where the plane was, that the field in Jacksonville would be marked with a white sheet, as usual.

The territory in this vicinity was quite wooded. Banning and Bill had to fly over forty miles of wooded land with no place to "set 'er down". They reached Jacksonville at the appointed hour. The sheet was in place, but there was no way in the world to land a plane in that small place without side slipping almost straight down, and to think of flying the ship out was preposterous. But the boys had figured on landing in Jacksonville, and didn't have gasoline enough to fly back to Corsicana, so they had to land in there, and in that small spot which was the only place in town or near town to land. By careful maneuvering Banning set the ship down on that field without running into the fence, but he called Taylor everything he could think of, for Taylor was so wrapped up in the fact that all his relatives would see the plane that he paid no attention to the field.

The boys learned a great lesson from this—that an advance agent for aeronautical affairs should unquestionably be a pilot, in order to select a field with the proper location as to terrain, wind direction, obstructions, etc. Now how were they to get the plane out of that field? If it was not flown out they would have to remove the wings and cart it sixty-five miles to an open space large enough to take off from. But a farmer adjoining the lot on which the plane was located said that the fence could be removed, providing it was put back, so several men volunteered to help re-erect the fence after the plane should have taken off. But this additional run-way, made by razing the fence, was still short. However, Banning thought he could take off O.K.

The motor was revved up, and several men were put on each wing to hold until the tail of the ship was raised off the ground by the propeller blast. At a signal from Banning they let go, and the ship bounded down the rough runway. It finally raised off the ground. About 100 feet ahead were high lines about thirty feet from the ground. Just before reaching these lines the motor quit. Banning could have let the plane settle to the ground then, but in doing so he would have landed in the midst of several automobiles full of women and children who were watching the take-off. So he pulled the nose of the ship up and stalled it over the wires. Just over the wires he nosed it down to gain speed to pull up over another line of wires a few feet ahead. He barely made this second line of wires, and, just as the tail of the ship cleared, the ship stalled and came down nose first into a farmer's chicken house. The plane was practically a washout

but Banning was not hurt, not a scratch. The damages
to the chicken house and a peach tree that was rooted
up were estimated at $100, which had to be paid the
farmer.

This put an end to the barnstorming in Texas.
What next? Bill returned immediately to Los Angeles.
Banning remained in Dallas, Texas, fell in love with
Mable Norford and was married.

Betts and Allen were surprised to know that Bill
had returned to Los Angeles, especially after Betts
had written that Bill had run off and no one knew of
his whereabouts. But Bill was not the kind to give up.

Of the nine members of the Operations Group there
was only one man, besides Bill, who was willing to continue to work. He was Irvin Wells. Marie Dickerson
was willing, but she was leaving in a few days to
motor to New York to fill a theatrical engagement.
Lottie Theodore had arrived in Los Angeles while the
boys were lost in Mexico. She, too, was ready to carry
on. All the old members of the Executive Group
dropped out except Miss Corona White.

So, in the face of all these setbacks Bill, Wells, and
Lottie Theodore planned to carry on. Bill was broke,
but Wells had enough money to purchase a training
ship, which he did immediately, and they selected several more fellows and started training them. Under
the tutorship of Bill, these flyers made remarkable
progress secretly, and it was the greatest surprise to
Betts and Allen when they learned that the Bessie
Coleman Aero Clubs would stage the first All-Negro
Air Show on Labor Day, 1931.

And so on Labor Day 15,000 people turned out to
see an exhibition which astonished everyone. Banning
arrived from Texas just in time to participate. He was
also surprised to see four flyers exhibit: William
Aikens, Matthew J. Campana, Maxwell Love, and Lottie Theodore.

So with Bill, Banning, Marie—who was in New

York— and J. B. Hensley, who had just been added
to study the mechanical end, the group only lacked
two of having the ten to start out to Chicago to see
Rev. Braddan pay off.

The show went off exactly as scheduled. There
were no accidents and the people were well satisfied.

THE FIRST AIR SHOW

The main feature of the show was the dropping of a
wreath of roses by the Goodyear blimp, Volunteer, in
honor of Bessie Coleman.

The news of the success of this show spread, but
was given no added impetus by Betts through his
newspaper connections. Nevertheless Bill and Wells,
who had put it over, were elated. Their first air show
was a tremendous success.

CHAPTER X

The success of the first air show spurred Bill and Wells on. They could now boast of having the first Negro Formation Flying Group in America. This trio included Bill, Wells, and Aikens. Maxwell Love and Lottie Theodore were doing some wonderful parachute work and were progressing steadily in their flying also. Campana was getting to be a real stunt flyer. Banning, while he had not exactly quit the group, said that he was not going to spend his time helping to train others, and then, after all was said and done, be talked about and not given any credit for what he had done. So he said he would not do any work in the organization at all, but that he would fly any time, provided he was paid for it. Bill thought this was a pretty narrow stand to take, especially by Banning, because if anyone had benefited by the operations of the organization, it was he. Banning came to Los Angeles with his license expired. It was the organization that arranged that he might get time enough to be reinstated. Then, on top of that, he secured about 300 hours of flying at the expense of the organization. To purchase an equal amount of flying time a person would have to pay about $4,000.

But Bill was determined to fill the group. He had heard of three other flyers who were reported as doing very well. So he wrote to Leon Parrish, a West Indian in New York. Parrish answered that he was just getting ready to fly to Haiti with a white fellow and would not be available. Aviator James was doing some effective flying in and around New York. A letter was sent to him, but he went to his death stunting a plane in Gary, Indiana, before he could answer. Another letter was sent to Al Anderson in Philadelphia, who was busily engaged teaching.

Meanwhile, the success of the first air show was being felt in more places than one. Marie Dickerson in New York wrote that she would leave New York any time the group was ready to have another show or was ready to do any touring. A letter was also received from Colonel Hubert Julian, stating that he had read of the success of the group and that he congratulated them. He further stated that he had been promoted to the rank of Colonel while he was in charge of the Royal Abyssinian Air Forces in Abyssinia, and, since there were no aeronautical activities around New York for Negroes, he would like to cast his lot with this group, and help put the program over big. He stated that he had had over 1,000 hours of flying since he had seen Bill three years ago.

His letter at first surprised Bill, but, realizing that there were only a few Negroes actively engaged in aeronautics in America, he felt that if they all would combine their efforts, the objective would soon be reached. Notwithstanding the fact that Julian had been such a flop in Chicago, several years before, and overlooking the fact that he had never paid him for the automobile he drove away to Detroit, Bill felt, that, certainly now, being a colonel and having 1,000 hours to his credit, Julian would doubtless be an asset to the group and could do much to help the progress of the cause. So Bill accordingly presented the Colonel's name to the group. Everyone voiced objections, referring to unsavory rumors about the man. But Bill cited the fact that false rumors were out about himself. He then asked the group to give this man a chance. Finally they decided to do so, and the "Colonel" was voted in as a member.

Still another was needed to complete the ten. A young man named William B. Johnson, the husband of

Mrs. Frieda Shaw, prominent chorus directress in Hollywood, was chosen because he had followed the group activities everywhere and was extremely interested in learning to fly. This young man, Johnson, learned to fly quicker than any other member of the group. He seemed to be a born flyer.

The group of ten was now again completed, and, thanks to the generosity of Irvin Wells, equipment was on hand to complete their training. Bill again had dreams, depicting Rev. Braddan taking his dreaded airplane ride.

TRAINING FOR THE AIR SHOW
Martha Luke *(left)*, Myrtle Bishop *(right)*

The group training was progressing better now than at any previous time. The boys were ready to pull something big. The only thing standing in their way of flying to Chicago now was lack of airplanes. Bill wanted five planes so that the entire group could fly, two in each ship, in a "V" formation. He and Wells then began to plan some way to make the last step—to get five planes. They reasoned that first they must demonstrate the fact that they had five capable Negro pilots, and no better opportunity presented itself than an offer from the Associated City Employees

Fund for the Unemployed of Los Angeles to stage a Benefit Air Show. Up to this time, no Negro organization in Los Angeles had given a benefit for the general unemployed of the city, so this affair attracted much attention.

An idea struck Bill. They would feature Colonel Hubert Julian, the Black Eagle from Harlem, recent commander of the Royal Abyssinian Air Forces, in a thrilling Air Show with Bill's Five Blackbirds in formation flying. These names soon were on everybody's lips. Money was sent to Marie Dickerson in New York to defray the expenses of driving the Colonel to Los Angeles in her car.

But jealousy and envy seemed always to lurk around. Banning did not like the idea of featuring Colonel Hubert Julian. He felt he should be the feature, and so he refused to take a part. But Bill and Wells were determined to have five Blackbirds in the air on that date, and so the training of the other boys was doubled and Banning forgotten.

On the other hand, Thomas Allen, seeing the rapid progress of the group, now decided that he should get back with them. So he asked a certain member about getting reinstated. This member brought it up in the meeting, and Bill said immediately, "Nothing doing." The message carried back to Allen was that Bill was the cause of his not getting back in the group. So one night Allen went to the 20th Street School, where Bill usually attended a rehearsal of the Etude Ethiopian Chorus, and there waited for him. Twentieth Street is a very dark street at night, and when Bill arrived Allen sprang up with a four-by-four scantling and struck him a terrific blow. Luckily Bill raised his left arm and caught the blow, otherwise he would have had a crushed skull. Recovering from the surprise attack, Bill "lit" into Allen, who was much heavier than he, and each time he raised the club to strike, Bill rushed him with uppercuts and punches to the nose and mouth.

The third rush Bill knocked him down and took the club away from him, and was in the act of swinging on him when he broke loose, ran, and joined two other men in an automobile and sped away. In his haste he left his cap—which Bill now retains as a souvenir of the fight.

Little did Bill dream when he left his business in Chicago to take up aviation that he would have to fight as a part of the program! Surely Rev. Braddan knew what he was talking about when he said he would never ride in an airplane, yet would ride if Bill brought ten trained Negroes to Chicago at one time. But that was not the worst of it. Oliver Betts, the reporter who had failed to write up the success of the first Air Show, came out with a big article in a local paper to the effect that Allen had beaten Bill up and seriously disfigured him in a fight about aviation. This article was printed just a week before the approaching benefit air show. Having read it, Bill walked into the newspaper office and told the owner that he had just dropped in to let him know that they could not depend upon the truth of anything which Betts might say or write about him or the organization.

Marie Dickerson, Marie Daugherty, and Colonel Julian sped to Los Angeles in Mrs. Dickerson's car, stopping only at Chicago long enough for Julian again to contact Rev. Austin.

One would think that Julian's previous failures would have caused Rev. Austin to curse Negro aviation and have no more to do with it, but, to Julian's surprise, Rev. Austin invited him in and gave him quite an inspiring lecture on going forward in this field. The minister even carried Julian to the airport in his car, rented an airplane for the afternoon, and had Julian fly him and his daughter over Chicago. He then had him carry up his deacon and a trustee, all to prove to doubting Negroes that a Negro really could fly—a wonderful example of interest in Negro progress in industry.

Everything was being made ready for the big affair on December 6, at the Eastside Airport. Bill even arranged for the Mayor of Los Angeles to welcome Colonel Julian and Marie to the city on the steps of the City Hall, and so, on the date of their arrival, Mayor John C. Porter, Sheriff Biscailuz, and Supervisor John R. Quinn, honored our race by welcoming

CITY OFFICIALS WELCOME COL. JULIAN

Left to right (front row) Supervisor John R. Quinn, Sheriff Biscailuz, Marie Daugherty, Mayor John C. Porter, Col. Julian, Marie Dickerson, William F. Johnson

to Los Angeles the Negro's greatest flyer (as they all thought). It was a beautiful ceremony held on the steps of the City Hall. Bill, acting as master of ceremonies, introduced Mayor Porter when the Colonel and Marie arrived, after being rushed to the City Hall in a fine limousine. The Mayor made a very inspiring address of welcome. Then Bill introduced the Colonel, who really did honor to the race by his eloquent speech, which drew great applause from all, the white people especially. Then speeches followed by Supervisor Quinn, Sheriff Biscailuz, Dr. F. R. Whiteman, Commander of the Benjamin Bowie Post of the American Legion, Irvin Wells, Marie Dickerson, and Marie Daugherty. Music by the Police Band closed the ceremony, which was broadcast over station KECA. This ceremony marked the first time in the history of Los Angeles that a Negro had been received by the Mayor of Los Angeles on the steps of the City Hall, yet no mention was made of it by Betts or the local paper through which he had published his previous adverse reports.

The colored people on the East Side were all enthused over the coming event, and the response the group was receiving demonstrated that, with the proper showing, the advent of the Negro into the aviation industry would be only a question of time. Meanwhile, the Black Eagle and the Five Blackbirds were busily engaged practicing for the show.

About this time Julian met one of the belles of Los Angeles colored society, Miss Reverdia Woods, and started a whirlwind courtship with her such as he was then carrying on with about eight other girls in town. Miss Woods' mother was carried away with Julian's wonderful speech, manner, dress, politeness, etc.—she being most wonderfully impressed when the "Colonel" would put his English monocle over one eye and tell her that her daughter was "most chawming," and that she must give up her career as a dramatist and become an aviatrix to fly away with him—the Black Eagle of the Air.

He soon induced Mrs. Woods to purchase a beautiful flying outfit for her daughter—and she really was lovely in her uniform. The Colonel then started giving her flying lessons, which lasted only four days, because the owner of the training ship he rented refused to let him use the ship any longer after he had bent up the steel propeller and made about twelve landings by dropping the ship from eight or nine feet or more with a bang. Luckily it was a Fleet, for most training ships would have had a washed out landing gear with such treatment.

The great day of the big show came. Autos began to find their way to the field from all sections of the city, and from all the surrounding towns. Forty thousand people viewed the show. But the crowd was disappointed. They had featured the Black Eagle, but the Black Eagle didn't feature. Bill was much criticized

COLONEL JULIAN AND MISS REVERDIA WOODS

for giving the Colonel the spotlight when he could not produce. Banning, especially, was tickled to death at this. The Colonel was scheduled to make a triple parachute jump. He succeeded in making a single jump, but was very much peeved when he learned that the consensus of opinion was that Marie Daugherty had made a better jump than he. He was scheduled as the chief stunt flyer of the day, and held the crowd breathless watching him gain 6,000 feet altitude to perform hair-raising stunts which never materialized. He didn't even make a sharp bank, but soon descended, asking for a glass of water, stating that it was quite difficult to do all that hard flying and make a parachute jump also.

But the Blackbirds came to the rescue and saved the day. Now for the big surprise. The parade of the Blackbirds was next in order, and to the surprise of every one present seven Negroes took off in as many planes, one by one. This is the first time in history that seven Negro pilots were in the air together at one time.

Irvin Wells was the first to take off, flying a Challenger Commander. Then Bill Aikens followed in a Hisso-Eagle Rock. Next was Julian in a Fleet. Then William B. Johnson followed in a Waco 10. Campana followed in a Warner Travellaire. Marie Dickerson then took off amidst great applause in a Kari-Keen. Then Bill followed in a Wright J6 Travellaire. This was a wonderful sight for the colored people, just to see seven planes piloted by Negroes in the air at one time. The planes soon faded from sight. The plan was to fly to Vail Field, a few miles away, land, and then take off in formation and fly back over the exhibition field, do some maneuvers in formation, and then land.

Everybody landed on Vail Field except Julian. Even Marie, who had never landed on Vail Field before, shot a perfect landing there. All motors were kept running, waiting for the Colonel, but when he didn't show up Bill gave the signal and off they all went in "V" formation, with Marie trailing, making six planes together. Over Eastside Airport they came, first in "V", then in echelon, then trailing one another; then they split up, and each did his or her special stunt, and then landed on the field amidst the applause of the crowds. Then Maxwell Love and Marie Daugherty made stellar parachute jumps. The Blackbirds thus saved the day, and the crowd, after watching Frank Sebastian's Cotton Club entertainers, who furnished music for the afternoon, left well pleased. As the crowds were leaving, Colonel Julian returned to the field, stating that he got lost and went to the wrong airport, where he had waited for the bunch.

This show for the city's unemployed did much good. It demonstrated that the Bessie Coleman group was ready. All they needed was equipment. Notwithstanding the fact that Betts again failed to give the show any favorable publicity, a young writer for the Pittsburgh Courier sent through the news, and it appeared just the same in all the outstanding Negro papers. Julian, who made excuses for his non-performance, was nevertheless elated over the large crowd, and vowed he'd put his shoulder to the wheel and help put the program over in a big way. He then suggested that the next thing to be done was for a Negro to make a long flight, a transcontinental flight. This he said was necessary to show the people that Negroes were capable, and, after doing that, he said, it would be an easy matter to interest the proper people and so get equipment to carry on the work. All the members of the group thought that a good idea, so plans were laid to get a suitable plane for a transcontinental flight.

Julian stated that he had a Bellanca in New York, on which he had paid $30,000 down, but that he was going to use that for his across-the-ocean flight. He autographed a picture of this plane for everyone he came in contact with. So he contracted to purchase a Lockheed, stating that he would raise the balance of the money at a demonstration that he would give shortly. Members of the group didn't agree with this program, first because the plane he selected was obsolete, and secondly because he went on and made arrangements without even discussing the matter with any of the group. He accordingly advertised the christening of his transcontinental plane on February 22, 1932, at the Dycer Airport. The American Legion turned out and supported the affair wonderfully. Funds were raised, but they were not sufficient to pay for the plane. Bill suggested that he keep the money until more had been raised and then pay for the plane in cash; but Julian was positive he could raise the balance due within the sixty days allotted.

However, the Colonel failed to raise the money, and therefore lost all that was paid on the plane. He then made connections with a young widow in Los Angeles, Mrs. Reversta Tellis, who made the first payment of $500 down on another plane for him. This ship he

THE "REVERSTA TOLLERANCE"

named the Reversta Tollerance. He advertised that he would raise the balance of the money for it at a christening at which Mrs. J. B. Bass agreed to perform the ceremony. But Mrs. Bass failed to show up on the appointed day, and the collection was very small, so the Colonel lost another plane on which he had paid a considerable amount down.

However, the Colonel continued to send releases to the press that he would take off soon on a transcontinental flight, and, when told by the group that they did not like his actions of fooling the public, he resented it very much, and withdrew from the group.

But the public was now looking forward to a long distance flight by a Negro, and nothing else would please them. Several months passed and the Colonel had not yet taken off, so Irvin Wells suggested that he

and Bill get in the National Air Races which would
start August 27.

This was a great idea, for no Negro had ever entered a National Air Derby. But there would be some
of the best planes made, and some of the best pilots in
the country in these races. The training plane that
Wells had purchased for the group training was all
that was available. But Bill and Wells decided to tune
the motor up and enter the races with this plane, an
OX5 Lincoln Paige. It would at least demonstrate that
a Negro was capable of flying long distances, Wells
said.

There were fifty-six planes entered in the Pacific
wing. There was Jim Granger flying his J5 Swallow,
Gladys O'Donnell flying her Warner Monocoup, Eldon
Cessna flying a Warner Cessna, and a host of other
good pilots and ships. But Bill and Wells entered their
OX5 with great pride, and qualified their ship at an
average speed of 94.7 miles per hour—not so bad for
an OX5. Of course they did not expect to win, but the
experience to be gained was well worth the entry fee
and the cost of the gasoline and oil to Cleveland. That
night at the meeting of the group, Lottie Theodore
suggested that, after reaching Cleveland, Bill and
Wells should continue on to New York, and thus become
the first Negro transcontinental flyers. She said they
would be so near New York that they might as well do
this. So this suggestion was adopted. It was then decided that Hensley, the mechanic of the group, would
assist in overhauling the motor and installing a dual
ignition system. But the next day Hensley could not
be found. This was strange, because they had only a
week in which to get ready.

Nevertheless, Bill and Wells made the ship ready
for the races and qualified two days before the take-off.
All this time Hensley had not been heard from, but the
day before the take-off, a girl called Bill over the
phone.

"Hello, is this Bill?" the young lady asked. "I just called to tell you that Banning and Hensley are preparing and overhauling a plane in an effort to take off a day or so ahead of you for New York. They figure, since you and Wells are entered in the races and have to stop at the different control points, that they can start and go straight on to New York and be the first Negro transcontinental flyers. They have been at my house talking, and I thought it a very dirty trick, especially as I always thought they belong to your group."

This news stunned Bill. Not that he was afraid of these boys beating him to New York, nor did he care, so long as some Negro had made the flight, but the underhand way in which they went about it hurt him.

"If they could get a plane ready, it would be far better to have a race between two planes to be the first Negro transcontinental flyer. This would stir up more enthusiasm among members of the race than our entering the National Air Derby," said Bill to Wells, as they were on their way to Mines Field for the big take-off.

There were thousands of white people there to see the start of the big race, but only a few colored people. This was due entirely to the fact that they did not know that a Negro was entered in the race, as neither Betts nor any local paper with which he had any influence had given the matter any publicity, although they knew of it. However, all the members of the group were on hand to wish the boys good luck except Hensley and Banning—even the Colonel was there.

The first plane off was Leslie Miller's Nicholas Beasley. Then John Hardesty roared down the long runway. Then the white flag was placed between Mary Charles and Bill, as they were taking off at the same time. Down the runway these planes roared together. Presently they both rose from the ground, and, after passing the high lines, a sharp bank to the left—and Bill and Wells were headed for Yuma, Arizona, the first stop. Then in quick succession the planes took off, until all fifty-six were strung out on their way to Yuma.

The Lincoln Paige that our boys were flying was rigged for speed and not for climbing. Hence Bill had difficulty in getting altitude. Realizing that there were some pretty high mountains to cross if he set a direct course to Yuma, Bill decided to head straight for San Gorgonio Pass and then to Yuma. A gradual climb to an altitude of 3,000 feet by the time the plane passed over Riverside was sufficient to make the pass. Everything went fine. Wells kept check on the landmarks and the course so that no time would be lost at all. They passed March Field, then entered San Gorgonio Pass with just 500 feet altitude. Once through the pass, Wells indicated the course which led them down the left side of the Salton Sea. But was it hot? Their lips chapped. The desert heat was terrible. The water temperature in the motor ran up nearly to the boiling point, but on they went. After passing Palm Springs the air became cooler, due to the proximity of the Salton Sea. Leaving the Salton Sea behind, two other planes were seen closing in on Bill. These were the first planes they had noticed since leaving the bunch at Mines Field. Bill opened the throttle wide in an effort to keep the lead, but gradually the other planes gained until the airport at Yuma hove in sight. Bill was flying at 2,000 feet and both the other planes were flying at about 500 feet. About a mile out of Yuma, Bill nosed the OX down in a long glide, with the throttle wide open. The extra speed gained gradually carried him ahead of the two planes that had gained on him. Finally the white finish line was visible. Coming in at right angles to this line about 500 feet from the ground, Bill pulled the nose up in a steady climb, followed in close succession by the other two planes. It was a wonderful race. The first lap was over. Circling the field to the left they landed in the dust stirred up by the taxying of so many planes. And our boys were not the last ones in, as they figured they would be, according to the ship they flew. Many other planes were seen just coming in. And still they came, and some did not reach there at all.

Bill and Wells were greeted by Bob Hassell, Ursula Land, and Ray Davis. That night they were entertained at the residence of Mr. Cecil Hulit.

The next morning, Bill and Wells were at the field bright and early. They started the motor up to test its performance and found that their gas line was broken. Luckily they discovered it in time. They were to take off within a half hour. Some fast work, and Wells had annealed the gas line, pronouncing it O.K.

At 8:30 A.M., they were off again, this time on the second lap of the race to Tucson, Arizona. Leaving Yuma, the Mohawk Mountains loom up a short distance out. They had trouble getting their altitude as usual, but picking out the low spots, or passes, in the mountains, they went through. They were going along fine about an hour out of Yuma, when one cylinder began to miss. "This must be valve trouble", thought Bill, and he started to look for a place to set down, for he realized that the vibration caused by the uneven running of the motor might cause serious trouble before they reached Tucson. Lucky for them, they were over a wide, level field. Heading up-wind they made a perfect landing. Inspection of the motor disclosed that a valve was holding open, due to a broken valve spring. This spring was quickly replaced, and they soon took off again. Just before reaching Tucson, they passed near one of the ships in the race that had made a forced landing in a rough section. Soon they had landed on the airport at Tucson, and, to their surprise, several ships were not yet in. Not so bad, they thought, after having to stop and replace a spring. They had only a short time to take off for El Paso—forty-five minutes. So they gassed up, checked the oil and radiator, and got a few sandwiches. About fifteen minutes before take-off time, they started up the motor; the carburetor overflowed, and dense black smoke began to come out of the exhaust stacks. The motor was stopped, and examination of the carburetor showed that the float was leaking and full of gas. Tough luck; it would take some time to repair the float. There were no facilities to do this at the field, so they had to go to town and have it soldered. Two hours had passed before the carburetor was back on the plane and they were ready to take off. All the other ships had left long ago. It was late in the afternoon and there was doubt as to whether the boys would reach El Paso that night with the other flyers, after leaving so late. But they shoved off. Trouble lurked ahead. Black clouds were gathering right in their path. On they went, up three thousand feet, then four thousand, then five, six, then seven thousand feet up. It was very pleasant up there, nice and cool, and it was necessary to get that altitude because Dos Cabezas Range was looming up. Then, too, there was a tail wind up there. Passing over one range the boys noticed a rain storm directly ahead of them. They turned to go around it. Just as they were opposite this storm, another was seen closing in from the other side. Just then a few drops began to hit them in the face. Looking up, Wells noticed a big black cloud so low that he could almost reach his hand into it. A terrible sight! Rain on both sides, a black cloud only about ten feet overhead, altitude 7,000 feet, mountains 1,000 feet below. What a terrible sight! But straight ahead a ray of sunshine let them know that if they would keep going they would pull through all right. A wonderful lesson portrayed by nature itself! Yes, they would keep going.

It wasn't long before they had passed all clouds and the sun was shining all around them. But it was growing late and the sun was about to set.

They passed Lordsburg, and later on, Deming. The sun had just set. They had no navigation lights on the plane, which meant that they would not reach El Paso that night. Bill looked over his map. He decided that he could reach the emergency landing field at Mt. Riley within the next half hour, and so keep the Department of Commerce rules regarding navigation lights. About that time the rotating beacon at Mt. Riley began to operate. They flew straight for it. Just at twenty-nine minutes after sunset they landed at Mt. Riley, with the water in the radiator at the boiling point. The altitude of this emergency field is 4,300 feet, which called for a hot landing. Examination of the water connections for the cause of the boiling water disclosed the fact that two hose connections were leaking. Not having any extra hose connections, they wrapped the old ones with tape, trusting that it would hold until they reached El Paso, which was only forty miles away.

As there was not a town within five miles of this field, the boys decided to sleep in the ship all night and take off for El Paso early in the morning, in order that they might take off with the rest of the flyers on schedule time. Next morning early they took off from Mt. Riley, arriving at El Paso about 8:00 A.M.

The other ships were ready to take off. But Bill decided to put on two new water hoses and change oil. When this was done the motor failed to rev up to its usual R.P.M. They then tried to ascertain the cause of this drop in R.P.M. The magneto breaker points were checked, its synchronization with the distributor points was checked again and again. Spark plug gaps were checked. Valve clearances were checked. Finally, after nearly a whole day of checking the motor, she revved up to standard.

At 5:00 P.M. they decided to reach Roswell before dark, then at daybreak catch up with the rest of the flyers in order to move out with them on schedule next day.

About an hour out of El Paso the motor began to heat up again. They were over pretty rough country. There was no chance to set down. The motor began to lose revs fast. The Sacramento Mountains were no place to set a ship down. Bill jazzed the throttle. Probably it was not open all the way. 1600—1500—1400—1350—1300, and then 1200 R.P.M. This was not enough to sustain the Lincoln Paige in level flight. But when she dropped to 1150 R.P.M. there was nothing to do but look for a place to land. There was no place, the ship was slowly sinking, the mountains were coming up! Bill turned up wind—there was nothing to do but set 'er down somewhere, on a mountain slope, in a ravine—somewhere. Bill cut both switches, yelled to Wells to buckle his belt tightly, then, in the twinkling of an eye, he pulled back on the stick and stalled the plane onto a little knoll. But there was no place to roll, and the left wheel struck a boulder, the ship nosed over down the hill, landing on its back. In a second both boys were out of the ship, running up the hill, for fear it would catch on fire. A narrow escape! No one would ever believe that they landed that ship up there in the Sacramento Mountains without either getting a scratch. It soon would be dark. How far were they from a farmhouse?

CHAPTER XI

THE FLYING HOBOS

But, let us turn back to Los Angeles and see what is going on. You'll remember that Hensley disappeared, and it was discovered that he and Banning were working day and night on a motor to get it in condition to take off, and, taking advantage of the fact that Bill and Wells were in the Air Races, planned that they would fly right on into New York and be the first Negro transcontinental flyers.

They had much difficulty in raising funds to overhaul the motor of the OXX6 Eagle Rock owned by Arthur Dennis, who graciously loaned the boys the ship in an honest effort to aid Negro progress in aviation. Arthur Dennis (known as Small Black) in partnership with Sam Moore, purchased this plane for his own personal use, although he has never soloed. But he represents the first class of Negroes who will offer a potential market for airplanes—the sporting class, who always manage to purchase just about what they want.

Although the sporting class among Negroes are usually criticized by the other brethren for abstinence from the Church and things pertaining to religion, I must say here that they possess one thing that many professed Christians are lacking in—namely, that they are loyal one to the other. When the call went out from Small Black, who is one of the leaders of the sporting class on Central Avenue, there was little difficulty in raising four to five hundred dollars, in short time, with which to put the motor in condition—purchasing two scintilla magnetos, Miller overhead, steel propeller, compass—and for overhauling the motor, putting it in first-class shape for the trans-continental flight; yes, when Small Black called, Marie Daugherty got the girls and boys together, and they soon "chipped in" and raised the money.

The ship was therefore ready the day after Bill and Wells left with the racers, but Small Black noticed the progress of the Colored Derby plane and stopped preparation for the flight in his ship, stating that it seemed as though the other boys would make it all right.

But when the radio announced that Bill and Wells were forced down seventy-five miles east of El Paso, then Small Black consented to Banning's wishes to continue preparation for the flight. But gasoline and oil money now stood in the way. Small Black had raised the money to overhaul the ship and had furnished the ship, but would go no further. He told Banning that if he would raise gasoline money, he could go. For two weeks Banning tried in vain to raise gas money. Hensley, who had done most of the motor work, was broke also. He was scheduled to make the trip with Banning. Banning then sought aid from Marino, another aviation enthusiast and pilot, who referred him to Thomas Allen, who, he said, had sufficient funds to purchase fuel with.

So Banning went to Allen. Allen propositioned Banning that he would furnish gasoline and oil money, provided he could accompany Banning on the trip. Poor Hensley—he had worked hard day after day on the motor, and his nightly dream was of his flight to New York. But his dream turned out to be a nightmare, for Banning accepted Allen's proposition readily, which was no more than was to be expected, as Banning had previously declared that he was out for Banning and Banning alone.

By this time Bill and Wells had already returned to El Paso. When they were forced down in the Sacramento Mountains, they recalled having seen a farmhouse somewhere in the vicinity. But they had no idea in which direction to start, and walking in those mountains would certainly be a task. Hence Bill suggested that they rest until dark, at which time the lights in the farmhouse would come on, and then they could walk straight to the place (Bill certainly believed in lights!). His previous experience in the Mexican Desert served him well, for as soon as it grew dark the lights in several farmhouses about fifteen miles away showed up.

They started down the mountain side—over the rocks—through the ravines—around the cactus bushes with their thorns daring anyone to run into them. On they went into the night, with the stars shining brightly overhead. Now and then the howl of a coyote broke the silence. Soon the moon came out, and the picture presented reminded one of the glorious moon-shiny nights on the desert shown on the screen when the Foreign Legion marched through great sand dunes of the Sahara Desert—surely a writer could get wonderful inspiration on a night like this in such a place.

About midnight the lights seemed farther and farther away. The boys were tired. They lay down to take a short nap. Presently they were aroused by prairie dogs all around them. They got up and continued the march. An hour later they lay down again, with the same results, and so decided to continue on to the farmhouse. About 2:30 A.M. a dog began to bark nearby, letting them know that they were only a few steps from the farmhouse, the lights of which had long since been put out. They soon came upon a large ranch house, but decided not to disturb the owner at that hour of the night. So they lay down upon the sand and soon were fast asleep.

They were awakened next morning by the mooing of cows. The ranchman was up. When the boys told their story, the ranchman, a Texas ranger, did not believe it.

"You mean to tell me that you landed a plane up

in the Sacramento Mountains and didn't get hurt? Impossible," said he. "I never heard of a Nigger flyer anyway, and furthermore I believe youse are the two fellers that killed that milkman in El Paso night before last and that you are trying to disguise yourselves in flying suits."

But the boys immediately produced their flying licenses, which had their photographs on them. This satisfied the ranger temporarily. He was not the boss. The boss would soon be in from El Paso. So he gave the boys breakfast and watched them until a car drove up with four men in it. All of them had shotguns. Didn't look so good, but nevertheless the boys told their story again. These men didn't believe the story until pilot licenses were again presented.

But young McGregor, son of the ranch owner, who was himself a pilot, knew that these two boys were in the races. He saw them land in El Paso. He was extremely interested. He immediately persuaded the father and the rest of the party to go and find the plane. But not until they had cooked a good squab breakfast—the reason they had the shotguns was that they had been hunting.

And so Mr. Gibson McGregor, his son Douglas, Mr. Shannon Cook, and Mr. F. S. Brooks led the way back to the plane as far as they could by automobile, and then walked the rest of the way. The young rancher soon picked up the trails made by the boys the previous night and led the way to the plane. He took a picture of it. The men were as nice to the boys as they were interested. The elder McGregor put all conveniences at their disposal. The plane was dis-assembled a couple of days later and carted to El Paso for repairs and then re-assembled, as it was impossible to fly the plane out of such rugged country.

Mr. McGregor is one of the richest cattle men in Texas, owning 350,000 acres of land.

The El Paso dailies unstintingly praised the boys

for their ability to get down in those mountains, which is one of the toughest flying spots in America, and get out without a scratch.

The colored people of El Paso made the boys quite forget that they were out of the air races, for Professor W. O. Bundy and his son W. O. Bundy, Jr., Freddie Hughes, and William Brazier made things so pleasant for them that they hardly wanted to return to Los Angeles.

Jack Richards, a licensed airplane mechanic, was left in charge of the repairs on the plane.

Entering the National Air Races did much to stir up enthusiasm among the Negroes, for the progress of the Derby flyers was broadcast daily over the radio, and the white newspapers carried articles each day about the flights.

The Pittsburgh Courier, one of the largest Negro newspapers in America, scooped the country following the progress of the first Negro Air Derby flyers, and gave a detailed description of the flight. The Courier always welcomes the opportunity to print anything concerning the progress of the Negro race, especially along aeronautical lines. If all other Negro newspapers would follow the Courier's example, it would not be long before the Negro could boast of being in on the ground floor of at least one of the large industries.

Leroy Collins, a Negro Associated Press agent from Phoenix, Arizona, followed the progress of Bill and Wells in the air races, and rushed to El Paso and there photographed the wreck of the Air Derby plane. Returning to Los Angeles, he discovered that Banning and Allen were ready to depart for New York. He immediately suggested that for the best interest of the Negro in general, a race to New York between Banning and Allen in one plane and Bill and Wells in another would stir up a great deal of enthusiasm. So he wrote Bill not to continue on to New York after repairs on the Derby plane should have been completed, but instead, to return to Los Angeles for the race with Banning.

This idea struck Bill and Wells just right. They were for it. They were positive this would stir up an unusual amount of interest among the colored people, so they immediately returned to Los Angeles.

But the following day, when Bill went to Small Black to make arrangements and discuss plans for making the race effective, he learned that Banning and Allen had slipped out of town that very afternoon, en route to New York.

At first Bill was angered. Of course the honor of being the first Negro transcontinental flyer was not to be made light of, but after all, the same results would be accomplished regardless of who made the first transcontinental flight, just so it was a Negro, although they felt that a much larger chance was lost by not making it a race between the two planes.

Bill thought it a dirty trick, however, because he and Wells would not have returned from El Paso. They would have continued on to New York.

They decided then to watch Banning's time on the flight and later on fly across the continent and beat his record, their main idea being to arouse great interest in flying among their people.

Banning, the veteran Negro flyer in America, had nearly 800 hours of flying time, having acquired about 400 hours with the Bessie Coleman organization. He was a good stunt flyer and had two years of college training. It is no wonder that, as qualified as he seemed to be, people wondered why he possessed only a private pilot's license. Many theories have been advanced about this—some stated that although he was a good flyer, he didn't know the other subjects necessary to fit him to pass the required transport pilot's examination. Others stated that because he was a Negro, the Department of Commerce inspectors didn't give him a break. This idea was quite prevalent among Banning admirers, especially after the following episode:

One day Herman James, a Negro flyer, was going up for his transport pilot's examination. There was a white flyer who was to take his examination at the same time. Both boys had books, studying navigation and meteorology, just prior to the time when they would take their written tests. In front of several people standing around, the white pilot asked Herman what was a "rhumb line". He laughed and replied, "It is a line three miles out in the ocean, this side of which it is illegal to possess or sell rum." The white pilot thanked him for the answer and departed.

James then explained to his friends that he had misinformed the white pilot, and said that a rhumb line was really a line on the surface of a sphere which makes equal oblique angles with all meridians. This made James appear to be the best informed of the two pilots; but when the examination was finished, the white pilot passed and James failed.

Immediately a howl went up from James' friends, saying that race prejudice was the cause of his flunking. And the idea has spread among Negroes in various parts of America that they stand a very poor show of getting licenses, due to prejudiced Department of Commerce inspectors—many a young Negro turning away from aviation on this account.

This particular incident is mentioned to correct this idea, and to let the future Negro pilot realize that preparation, and not race prejudice, will govern his aeronautical activities.

James Banning was born in Canton, Oklahoma, November 5, 1900. He graduated from Faver High School in Guthrie, and spent two years at Iowa State College studying engineering. He became interested in aviation in 1925, and journeyed to Chicago, thinking that he could get into an aviation school there, but was turned down on account of being colored. After being rejected in Minneapolis, Kansas City, and St. Louis, he finally persuaded an Army officer, Lieut. Raymond Fischer of Des Moines, Iowa, to teach him to fly, and so, in 1926, when the Department of Commerce first started their license laws, we find Banning the only licensed Negro pilot in America.

The day they were ready to hop to New York, a discussion ensued between them. Allen deplored the fact that they didn't have enough money for gasoline and oil all the way to New York. They didn't have enough money for living expenses and for hangar rent for the plane. What would they do? But they both had plenty of nerve and were quite willing to take a chance on begging funds as they went along.

"Gee", said Allen, "we'll be just like hobos, begging our way."

THE "FLYING HOBOS"
Banning, Allen, and the first successful Negro Transcontinental Plane

"Fine", said Banning. "That gives me an idea. We'll capitalize on our plight. We'll call ourselves the 'Flying Hobos.' "

This was indeed a fitting name for them for they were dressed the part, their funds, also, were typical of the part, and even the ship they were flying was old

and antiquated, notwithstanding the fact that a few
hundred dollars had been spent to make it quite safe
for the transcontinental flight.

And so at 4:00 P.M. that afternoon our "Flying
Hobos" left Dycer Airport en route to New York to be
the first Negroes to span the continent by air.

Their ship, an OXX6 Eagle Rock, was in pretty
good condition. The motor ordinarily developed 100
horsepower—with the addition of two scintilla magnetos and a steel propeller a few additional "revs"
were added to help them clear the high ranges.

Due to the heavy fogs which had hovered over Los
Angeles for the three weeks previous to the flight, they
were forced to wait until afternoon to depart. Their
first flight was a journey of sixty miles to Arlington
Airport, where they remained for the night.

The next morning, leaving Arlington Airport, they
headed for Yuma, Arizona, via the San Gorgonio Pass,
leaving the San Jacinto Range and San Bernardino
Mountains behind them. Passing the Salton Sea, Yuma
soon hove in sight. This town was a very familiar
sight to Banning, who had spent several days flying in
this vicinity. Landing at the airport to refuel, an
attendant recognized Banning and said: "Say, aren't
you the same fellow who landed here two years ago
and blew out a tire?"

"Yes", said Banning.

"Well," he continued, "your accident is the cause of
us having a real airport now. You know the concrete
circle in the field was poorly made and kept, with a
sharp edge protruding, and when you made a three-
point landing right in the circle your wheel hit the concrete and tore off your tire. Well, we reported your
accident to the city and asked for an appropriation to
fix up the airport and got it. Some airport now, eh?"

"Yes", said Banning, "that should be worth at least
a tank of gasoline."

And soon they were headed toward Tucson, reaching there just before dark.

The next day at 8:00 A.M., they shoved off for El Paso, going through Apache Pass. At Lordsburg, New Mexico, gasoline was taken on. Late that afternoon they rounded the Franklin Mountains and landed at the municipal airport, El Paso.

Leaving El Paso, our "Flying Hobos" reached Midland safely. Over El Capitan Peak clouds engulfed them, causing them to fly blind for a few minutes. The Eagle Rock was then riding at 9,000 feet altitude. A few drops of rain heralded the approach of a storm which soaked the boys through. Sighting the Pecos River, they searched for a landing field, stopping at Wink, Texas, for the night.

The next morning they shoved off in cloudy weather. The day's flying was without incident. About 5:00 P.M., they landed at Wichita Falls, leaving the worst flying country behind them.

The next day they headed for Oklahoma City, Allen's home. They stopped at El Reno, Oklahoma, long enough to see Banning's brother and cousin.

The next stop of a few days was at Oklahoma City, where Allen had a chance to visit his home folks. Leaving Oklahoma City, they headed for St. Louis, but at Carthage had to land in a wheat field to adjust the valve action of the motor. At St. Louis they paused a few days to grind the valves.

Soon they were on their way via Terre Haute, Springfield, and Columbus. Stopping at Columbus a few days, they set out for Pittsburgh to visit the Pittsburgh Courier, but were forced down at Cambridge. After repairs they again set out for Pittsburgh, where they were most royally welcomed and entertained by Editor R. L. Vann, W. E. Hance, and Ira F. Lewis.

A few days later they headed for New York, passing over Johnstown, Harrisburg, and Philadelphia. They stopped over night at Trenton.

The next day, Sunday, October 9, 1932, our "Flying Hobos" landed at the Valley Stream Airport, New York, the first Negroes to span the continent by air—although it was three weeks from the time they started, their actual flying time was a little over forty-one hours—and thus history was made for the Negro, and a mark was set up for other Negroes to shoot at. A transcontinental flight by a Negro was an accomplished fact, and fitting tribute should be paid these "Flying Hobos," as they styled themselves, for their nerve, for their daring, for their endurance in spanning the country under the conditions which they encountered.

In New York they were accorded a hero's welcome, but the writer is of the opinion that not enough significance has been given this flight by Negroes: for, if such a creditable showing can be made with limited training and inadequate and antiquated equipment, there remains no doubt that with proper training and equipment the Negro can take his place along side all others in the aeronautical field.

The "Flying Hobos" demonstrated this without a doubt, as did Bill and Wells, who had the audacity to compete in the National Air Races against some of the best ships in America, with a plane which did not even equal the power rating and ceiling of the Eagle Rock used by Banning and Allen.

After the New York reception, our "Flying Hobos" were the guests of the Editor of the Pittsburgh Courier, Robert L. Vann, who arranged financially to have a new motor installed in the transcontinental plane— a Wright Whirlwind J5. This installation put the ship in first-class condition, and so the boys planned to tour the United States, giving a series of exhibitions to arouse the Negro to flying.

But misfortune overtook them on their way to

Pittsburgh en route to stage a great exhibition. They did not reckon with a head wind in their path, and consequently ran out of gasoline on a short trip of 150 miles, which was equivalent to 225 miles as far as gasoline consumption is concerned, due to the stiff wind retarding their progress.

They had to make a forced landing, damaging one wing of the plane very badly in the attempt. This really set them back. They ordered the plane repaired and went on to Pittsburgh and used another plane in the exhibition at Bettis Field.

However, not enough money was raised to pay the cost of repairs on the plane (four hundred and fifty dollars). So they journeyed to Los Angeles by bus, to raise funds to secure the release of the plane, which was being held for the repair bill.

The first Negro transcontinental flyers, the first Negroes to span the continent by air, the first Negroes to prove to members of their own race and to members of other races that a Negro could fly across the continent—what a reflection on the Negro race—their plane was held for a repair bill of less than five hundred dollars, even before news of the epochal flight had been widely spread.

And no organization, no group of Negroes, appreciated the sacrifices, the daring, of these two young men enough to sponsor raising the $500 to pay the repair bill, in order that they might continue their campaign to arouse Negroes to a future industry full of commercial possibilities.

Broken-hearted, but still determined to carry on, they planned a series of exhibitions and lectures on the West Coast.

But the wrath of God waxed strong. He was angered, not at the coast-to-coast-flyers, but at a race of people so ungrateful, so unmindful of good deeds performed. They must pay. And they must pay dearly for such gross negligence.

Banning and Allen, under the management of John B. Hensley, staged an exhibition at the Eastside Airport in Los Angeles. Another exhibition was scheduled for San Diego the following Sunday. On Wednesday, Bill received a phone call: "Hello, Bill, this is Banning. I just called to see if you were home. I'll be right over."

Presently Banning rang Bill's door bell, and after talking at length about the transcontinental flight, Banning said to Bill: "Well, Bill, Allen and I have split; he won't be in San Diego with me Sunday. I'd like for you to come down and fly with me. After all, Bill, we have worked together for a long time and our association has always been agreeable. Seems as though we understand each other. I have often regretted that such a trifle as headlining Col. Hubert Julian at an air show should have caused me to break away from you. I missed you terribly on the transcontinental flight."

"Yes, Banning," Bill replied. "It is indeed too bad. I guess you and I know more about this game than any of the rest of the fellows, and there's no question about it, we should be working together at all times. I was a bit hurt when you fellows slipped out on us on the transcontinental flight, especially since Wells and I came all the way back from El Paso in order that the two planes might race across the country. But, after all, I am glad you made it—you deserve it. You are the first Negro licensed by the United States Department of Commerce, and you have the greatest number of flying hours, and you should have been the first Negro to span the continent."

"Thanks", said Banning, "then let's shake and get down to the old plans, for there is much work ahead of us, and this cross-country flight has convinced me more than ever that young Negroes throughout America are very anxious to learn aeronautics."

And so Bill agreed to accompany Banning to San

Diego, thus patching up the sore spot between the two outstanding Negro aviators in America. But it rained all Saturday and Sunday, hence there was no chance for the exhibition, which was postponed a week.

The following Sunday it again rained, and the exhibition was postponed for the second time.

The third Sunday, Bill, Wells, and Maxwell Love made ready to motor to San Diego early in the morning, but to the disappointment of all concerned, it rained for the third consecutive Sunday.

"Gee," said Maxwell Love as the rain poured down, "seems as though that exhibition at San Diego is doomed for bad luck."

Bill said nothing. A queer feeling came over him. He would not be able to accompany Banning the next Sunday, for he was engaged to sing in an operetta at church.

The following Friday, Bill expressed his regrets to Banning because he could not assist in the San Diego exhibition.

"Yes", said Banning, "I'm very sorry, too," and he gave Bill a picture of himself and Allen standing in front of the transcontinental plane.

That Sunday was unusually clear, probably because God was smiling and pleased that He had at last found a way to pour his wrath upon an unmindful race—yes, for three weeks He had pondered over it, for three weeks it had rained, and this day, February 5, 1933, God poured forth his wrath upon a people by calling to rest the best flyer of the race, the first Negro licensed by the United States Department of Commerce, the first Negro transcontinental flyer—James Herman Banning—for just as the plane Banning was to fly at the exhibition at Camp Kearney Field was to be made ready for him at Lindbergh Field, a Navy flyer (white) volunteered to fly Banning over to Camp Kearney Field to see how the crowd was coming. There were no controls in the front cockpit where Banning was sitting. Having seen a large crowd assembled on the field, the flyer started back to Lindbergh Field with Banning in the front cockpit. Probably this flyer wanted to show Banning that he, too, was a stunt flyer, because he "gave 'er the gun", gained a short distance across the field, then pulled the nose of the ship up into a steep climb. It was too steep. There was no possible chance of escape. The plane stalled and fell off into a spin, carrying Banning to instant death in front of all the spectators. The plane was not high enough for him to use a parachute and jump. And so the race paid dearly.

Surely the sacrifices of this pioneer, his daring, his courage, his ability, his determination to inspire the Negro to a new field of industry, shall be a great awakening, a great stimulus to the Negro in aviation.

CHAPTER XII

"The race is not given to the swift or the strong,
But unto him who endureth to the end."

Bill was determined not to be outdone. He was determined that there should be a wholesale awakening of Negroes in America in aviation. Several good offers had been made him individually in the aviation field. Two large airports in Los Angeles wanted to employ him to carry passengers in order to attract Negro trade. Arlington Airport in Riverside County offered him a job. Several groups offered him positions as instructor, and in one instance he was given a very nice offer to head an aviation school in Los Angeles. He received telegrams from a group of Jewish people in New York who wanted him to head a school for Negroes there.

But Bill contended that the few licensed Negro aviators in America should not pin themselves down to a job in some remote spot, but should dedicate themselves to spreading an interest in aviation among Negroes throughout America. He believed that the Negro unemployment situation could be wiped out if the Negro would get into some infant industry, and of course, aviation was the only such industry open. He wanted to see various groups of Negroes touring the country, carrying the message to other Negroes, giving air exhibitions, demonstrating the practicability and the safety of the airplane, and showing them the many opportunities in the aviation industry.

So, while the group training progressed steadily, each member was asked to bring in suggestions as to the best method of stirring up interest. About this time, Miss Myrtle R. Bishop, who had been making great strides in her aeronautical training, called Bill over the phone about 6:30 one morning.

"I'm very sorry I called you so early Bill, but I'm so excited; I haven't slept since midnight. I must talk to you just as soon as possible," she fairly shouted.

Well, thought Bill, what could be the matter now? Miss Bishop was one of the strongest members of the group, her whole heart and soul being wrapped up in stimulating aviation interest in her people. A thousand thoughts ran through his head as he drove to her house. To lose Myrtle from the group would mean the loss of its most diligent worker.

When Bill drove up to Miss Bishop's home he did not have to ring the bell, for she was outside waiting for him.

"I have an idea," said she, as Bill stepped out of the car.

"Good morning", said Bill.

"Along with our air exhibitions we could give a play that would convey our message better than lecturing", she continued.

"How are you this morning?" retorted Bill, a bit peeved. Is that what she disturbed me for so early in the morning?, he thought.

"Aw, good morning, I'm fine, and how are you, and I'm not joking either. I really believe it would be a much better way to put over our message, if we wrote a play and presented it—lectures are so dry, you know. We could give our air exhibitions during the day in various cities and schedule the play at nights at churches, halls, theaters, and so forth", she said angrily, a bit depressed because Bill did not readily warm up to her idea.

"By George", said Bill, "that sounds like it has some merit. Then write a play, Miss Bishop, and we'll see how it clicks."

"But you know I can't write a play, Bill; you do it."

"I never tried to write anything," Bill said, not a bit too cheerfully, as he still thought about the hours of sleep he had missed by being called so early.

"Oh, just write a play expressing our message to the public, add some music for entertainment and make it a little dramatic."

But Bill thought no more about it that day. That night, however, the idea of the play struck him quite forcibly. He immediately grabbed his Corona and started typing. For two days and nights he would not be disturbed, so busy was he writing the play.

On the third day the group was assembled to hear it read. It was written to include the entire group of ten. It was a story of an up-to-date Negro family whose educated children sought vainly for employment commensurate with their education. The three college children were always objects of ridicule to their good-for-nothing brother, who boasted that he was glad he didn't waste his time in college and then have to come out and accept a job as a porter. This ridicule continued until the depression brought on the loss of the home. The situation is finally saved through the many researches of the oldest son, who discovers an industry they might get into and build their own destinies— that industry was aviation. All the children finally get to California and enter an aviation school, and the good-for-nothing boy becomes a transcontinental flyer, makes a lot of money and redeems the home.

The members of the group thought the play O.K. and began immediately to learn their lines. After a few weeks of rehearsal, it was scheduled first at Beth Eden Baptist Church, under the auspices of group No. 4, of which Mrs. Elizabeth Price was president. No one in the group really thought the play was anything extraordinary. They looked upon it as just another play; all but Miss Bishop, who was enthused beyond words. "You'll see", said she, "it'll captivate the country and put over the message as nothing else could."

The night of the play came. Many people gathered more or less through respect for their friends in the cast. None really thought they would be entertained. As Mr. Hart, the representative of the Western News Syndicate, put it, he "came out to be bored".

But at the end of the first scene, as if fired by magic, the crowd was in a frenzy. Round after round of applause filled the auditorium as the members of the group unfolded their message, and a new inspiration was born in the breast of every Negro present that night.

The play was a great success. Bill was besieged for dates at nearly all the large churches. The press got busy. They heralded the story from coast to coast.

Surely the name, "Ethiopia Spreads Her Wings", given the play by Floyd C. Covington, was inspired, because from this date on Negro aviation took on a new impetus. The West Coast Negroes began to stir. The airports reported a tremendous number of Negroes taking airplane rides and many inquiring about flying lessons. Youngsters began organizing model clubs. The news spread to various parts of the country simultaneously. In Chicago the Challenger Aero Club received new life. They acquired an airport at Robbins, Illinois, a little Negro town fifteen miles from Chicago. They built a hangar. One of its members, Miss Janet Waterford, purchased a plane. The club membership was increased. The president of the club, Col. J. C. Robinson, got his flying license. Other members of the club pledged themselves to complete their training in order that they might stimulate interest in aviation among Negroes. They began their training in earnest to get ready to tour the country.

At about the same time, as if by mental telepathy, the East Coast received the message, for in Atlantic City, N. J., professional and business men, headed by

Dr. Albert E. Forsythe, organized a National Negro Aeronautic Society. This group defines aviation accomplishments as instruments to break down prejudices between nations, and to establish over night boundless good will; and the economic and scientific development in aerial transportation which results from these accomplishments defies all attempts at evaluation. Armed with these facts and backed by the Chamber of Commerce of Atlantic City and the Mayor of that city, this Society sponsored a good will round trip transcontinental flight.

In a Fairchild cabin monoplane, christened *The Pride of Atlantic City*, C. Al Anderson, a Negro transport pilot of Bryn Mawr, Pa., and Dr. Albert Forsythe of Atlantic City, left Monday, July 17, at 2:20 A.M. E. D. S. T., en route to Los Angeles on this good will flight.

"Ethiopia Spreads Her Wings"—the entire nation takes notice. The two daring Negro pilots left Atlantic City and were forced down at Camden, N. J., by fog. But they again took off, stopping to refuel at Harrisburg, Pittsburgh, Columbus, Indianapolis, St. Louis, Kansas City, Wichita, Amarillo, Albuquerque, Winslow, and Kingman. At Baldy Mesa they were forced down by an overheated motor. The crowd assembled at Grand Central Airport, Los Angeles. Bill and the group waited patiently for the arrival of these Negro good will flyers.

"Ethiopia Spreads Her Wings"—Negroes representing all walks of life were waiting on that air field. Never before had such interest and enthusiasm been manifested. There was Percy Buck representing the fraternal organizations and Elks Lodge; there was Clarence Johnson representing organized labor and the credit unions; Hartley Jones representing the Liberty Building Loan Association; Mr. and Mrs. Robert Dingee furnished their commodious car to transport the flyers through the streets of Los Angeles; Mrs.

Nellie V. Conner was there, representing business women of Los Angeles as well as placing her beautiful automobile at the disposal of the flyers during their entire stay in Los Angeles; Reverend Henry Gant represented the ministers; the Press was represented by many, and it was quite amusing to see the many members of the Negro press struggling to "scoop" something—Harry LeVette covered the event for the Associated Negro Press, Landis Buford for the Western News Syndicate, Lawrence LaMarr for the Pittsburgh Courier, and Leon Washington for the local press.

"Ethiopia Spreads Her Wings"—Floyd C. Covington represented the Urban League and declared that the work of Bill's group was Urban League work and that the play told the Urban League story better than he could tell it—therefore, he decided to give all his spare time and energy toward the promotion of this great work.

Clarence Muse, the great Negro motion picture and radio star, was there in the front ranks, as was Paul Williams, noted Negro architect—there were many other prominent persons there, too many to mention —all having caught the spirit of "Ethiopia Spreads Her Wings".

Presently, a little boy shouted "there they are", as he pointed towards the East. All eyes strained in that direction, and in a short time a beautiful cabin monoplane circled the field twice and glided gracefully down onto the large runway at the Grand Central Air Terminal.

Yes, they were there, for as the plane came closer and closer all could see that the pilots were Negroes. Everyone began to applaud, to yell, to whistle. Automobile horns joined in the noisy frenzy to welcome these Negro flyers, these intrepid birdmen who were the first Negroes to span the continent from East to West. Like veteran pilots they taxied their plane up the runway to where the crowd was surging back and forth behind the fence barrier. Bill was the first to greet the flyers. Then there was a mad rush. Cameras clicked. Everybody tried to get close enough to get a good glimpse of these men. Children were trampled on in the mad rush. Women fainted. It took Bill nearly an hour to get the crowd back and quieted long enough to carry through the welcoming ceremony planned by the group.

"BLACK WINGS" GREET THE HEROES
Left to right—Bill, Al Anderson, Myrtle Bishop, Dr. Albert E. Forsythe, Lottie Theodore, Gladys Wells, Floyd C. Covington.

Speeches of welcome were made by various prominent citizens of Los Angeles. The manner in which the heroes responded reflected their seriousness of purpose and their earnest desire to put over this great cause. They considered their feat nothing extraordinary, but as a necessary occurrence to aid in stimulating interest in this wonderful field. These men again proved that they were real heroes when Dr. Forsythe stated that, even in spite of the fact that they did not raise sufficient money to purchase the parachutes, landing lights, and instruments necessary and essential to blind flying, and despite the fact that they had no radio, they made the flight just the same to keep faith with the public. The applause which rang out at this point was deafening.

After the welcoming ceremony, the flyers were whisked away to the 28th Street Y. M. C. A., where they rested a short while. That evening they were banqueted at a reception given by the Eastside News Shopper and Bill's group. Early the following morning they were with Clarence Muse in his breakfast hour broadcast over Station KNX. Bill Sharples' questions over the microphone drew out the flyers' personalities, showing them to be the kind of leaders needed to sponsor great things in the race. Later in the day they broadcasted again over KNX, KFWB, and KRKD.

They were welcomed and received by Hon. Frank Shaw, Mayor of Los Angeles, in a broadcast over two stations. That night they flew over the American Legion March and later spoke to that gathering. Later in the evening they were the guests of Bill's group at a presention of the play "Ethiopia Spreads Her Wings". They pronounced the play wonderful, stating that they had received added inspiration and enthusiasm.

Friday morning, July 21, a large crowd assembled at the airport to see these heroes take off to complete their round trip transcontinental flight. They were scheduled to leave at 10:00 A. M. The motor was checked, the gas tanks filled, the course plotted. Everything was ready for the take-off within five minutes. These two boys worked together like clock-work. There was only one occasion that they were heard to disagree with one another, and this little argument occurred because, as Al Anderson told Bill the night before, the only fault he found with Forsythe was that he seldom thought about eating when there was something to be done. Just as they were all ready for the take-off, a beautiful young lady admirer came forth with a large basket of fruit and lunch. Dr. Forsythe accepted it graciously. After the lady had merged with the crowd, Forsythe reached into the plane for the box.

"What are you going to do with it?" Al asked, quite perturbed.

"Oh, I'm going to leave it with Bill, as it adds too much extra weight," replied Dr. Forsythe.

"Land's sake, no!" yelled Anderson. "Don't leave it. We can eat it on the way, the weight won't matter, it's only about seven pounds."

"But, Al, you know we've got to get over the hump very soon, and every pound counts," said the Doctor.

"Yes, but don't leave those eats behind! I'll get the ship over the hump all right."

But just at this time the young lady appeared again to bid them a last farewell, and Dr. Forsythe was forced to put the basket back into the plane. Bill is still wondering whether they threw the basket overboard later, or whether Al consumed the contents to lessen the load.

As the time for the take-off approached, the crowd wanted to get over the wire fence or break through the gate and come out on the field where the boys were with the plane. One man, Thomas Allen, who accompanied James Herman Banning on the first West to East transcontinental flight made by Negroes, succeeded in getting through the gate onto the field. He was accosted by Clarence Muse, who tried to eject him. "We're trying to keep everybody off the field to avoid accidents," said Muse to Allen. "It's the rule of the field anyway", he continued.

"Aw—I know everybody on this field," replied Allen boastfully, "You know I'm the first Negro transcontinental flyer."

With this remark Allen rushed past Muse, out to the plane. By this time Forsythe had just about completed charting his course, and he and Bill started from the hangar toward the ship.

The crowd of people had followed Allen's example, and had rushed out past Muse and was crowding out to where the ship was stationed. Suddenly there was a commotion. Allen had bumped into and broken off the gasoline gauge on the left wing tank of the transcontinental plane. Gasoline began to stream out of the tank. Maxwell Love, parachute rigger in Bill's group, rushed over and put his hand over the hole, holding back the gasoline as much as possible. The gasoline trickled down his sleeve and down his trousers leg. Later in the day he had to be treated at the hospital for gasoline burns and blisters.

Consternation ran riot in the crowd. Clarence Muse started for Allen. "Damn him", said Muse, "I tried to keep him off the field, let me at him." And it was all that several men could do to hold Muse off Allen. The crowd was put off the field while the hole in the tank was repaired. There was no gasoline gauge of that type available at the field so the boys had to take off with no gauge on the left wing tank. However, the hole was repaired in one hour and thirteen minutes.

And so, at 11:13 A.M., P.S.T., they took off and headed their monoplane toward Atlantic City. They were escorted a short distance out by two large planes carrying thirteen Negro passengers.

"Ethiopia Spreads Her Wings"—these good will flyers were entertained in Chicago by the Elks Lodge. They arrived in Atlantic City, Friday, July 28th, at 6:55 P. M., E.D.S.T. A large group, Negroes and whites, headed by the Mayor, Director of Public Safety and other city officials and prominent colored leaders of various organizations, gave them a tremendous ovation. Representing the colored citizens, Dr. Stanley Lucas, member of the Atlantic City Board of Education and Officer of the Board of Health, and Isaac Nutter, attorney, presented the flyers to Mayor Bacharack and Commissioner Cuthbert. The Mayor greeted the flyers warmly, congratulating them on their remarkable achievement, and stated that this was the first round trip transcontinental flight ever made by

any aviator of Atlantic City. After other speeches by
prominent citizens, the Mayor then presented each
flyer with a medal in appreciation of what the flight
meant to the city.

Forsythe and Anderson then responded to the
Mayor, thanking him for the medals and stating that
they were overwhelmed by the wonderful ovation they
had received. They also mentioned the fact that all
along the route of the flight great interest had been
shown in the project and a better interracial under-
standing had been brought about.

"Ethiopia Spreads Her Wings"—In Los Angeles
white aviation schools, seeing the interest being manifested by Negroes in aviation, opened their doors to
Negro students. Reports come in from all over the
country that the best white aviation schools are now
welcoming Negro students. Bill received many calls
from various airports inquiring for qualified Negro
mechanics and pilots . . . white air circus companies
getting ready to barnstorm the country sought Negro
flyers for their main attraction. Negroes all over
America are taking notice. Even Negro babies in their
cradles caught the spirit for as airplanes whirred
over head they looked up and tried to talk.

"Ethiopia Spreads Her Wings"—A group of women
in Los Angeles, realizing that there are hundreds of
young Negroes who would get into aviation if they had
the finances, have organized a National Negro Aviation
Aid Society, the purpose of which is to raise funds by
giving entertainments, such as teas, dances, bridge
parties, and other novel affairs, funds from which
will be used to sponsor worthy aviation projects among
Negroes, and to make it possible for young Negro men
and women to get into the aviation industry. These
women have set up an executive group, which in turn
is organizing units all over the country. This Executive Board is composed of Miss Katherine Payne, Mrs.
Irene Givens Freeman, Mrs. Mary Lassiter, Mrs. Car-

rie Fryerson, and Mrs. Lula Powell, with headquarters at 1259 West 36th Place, Los Angeles.

The first unit established by this group is headed by Mrs. Margie George; other officers of the group are Miss Azalia Black, Miss Louise Johnson, and Miss Effie Green. It is known as the Los Angeles West Side unit.

The awakening of the Negro in aviation, the spreading of Ethiopia's wings, is probably best signified in this letter received by Bill's group after the performance of their play in honor of the transcontinental flyers. A young man from Santa Monica, California, having seen the play, wrote as follows:

Black Wings Aviation Association,
4016 Central Avenue,
Los Angeles, Calif.

Gentlemen:

I am enclosing a poem that I wrote after having been inspired by your performance Thursday evening, July 20th, of "Ethiopia Spreads Her Wings", given at Miles Memorial Playhouse of this city. The theme and thought behind the play was wonderful. In my humble capacity may I offer the author and the association my sincere congratulations and also present them this poem entitled "Black Wings", written and expressly dedicated to Negro flyers of to-day and the glorious days to come.

And I should like to add that my interest in aeronautics dates back over several years; I was once enrolled for Army air service at March Field in 1927, but refused when they saw my face—it was then that I began to take the "game" seriously; I attended evening High School classes conducted by engineers of the Douglass Aircraft Co., for two years; I have been a contributor to the National Advisory Committee for Aeronautics at Washington, D. C.; and have flown several times as experimental aerial photographer. I hope to really some day accomplish something worth while in the field of aeronautical designing, therefore this interest in the efforts of your association.

I wish the Black Wings Aviation great future success.

Very truly yours,
VERNON F. S. BRUNSON.

BLACK WINGS

(Dedicated to Negro Flyers of to-day and the glorious days to come)

There's a sound of wings on the wind,
A faint, far, hum swells to a din—
Down from the heights a shadow flings;
It is the shadow of "Black Wings".
A new day's dawning in the sky.
Oh, ye who're earthbound heed the cry;
Oh, youth, come forth with brain and hand
To help these wings increase their span.
Come not with trembling steps and fears;
Heed not companion's warning jeers—
For they will have little cause for glee
When you have built an industry.
"Black Wings", dark as the sable night—
Wings, symbolic of strength and might
Are fluttering to awaken a race,
To rise and take its destined place.
All ways are closed except the sky.
Oh, race, to live, you've got to fly!
Now is the day to start, to climb—
To mold your wings, to fly with time;
Spread Ethiopia's pinions
Over all this world's dominions—
'Til all the earth your triumph sings
And skies are filled with swift "Black Wings".

And so at last we find Bill penning the following letter to Rev. Braddan:

Rev. William S. Braddan,
5810 Wabash Ave.,
Chicago, Ill.
My dear Reverend:

First let me congratulate you on your recent promotion to the grade of Lieut. Colonel. Since you are the first Negro to achieve that rank as a Chaplain it is quite commendable.

But now let me inform you that the Black Wings Aviation Association composed of twelve young men and women trained in various branches of aeronautics are preparing to fly in formation to Chicago to see you *pay-off*, by taking your first ride in an airplane. It was a hard job, but it is glorious to know that after all is said and done, Negroes *will stick together and do things*, and that Ethiopia is preparing to Spread Her Wings and soon the air will be filled with *swift black wings*.

Sincerely,
BILL.

"OPPORTUNITIES"

*A personal word
with the Author*

CHAPTER XIII

OPPORTUNITIES IN AVIATION FOR NEGROES

It is my frank opinion that Negroes, either young or old, do not have the slightest idea about the various opportunities open to them in aviation, for, if they had I am sure that in spite of depression and other hindrances, hundreds of Negroes would be qualifying along these lines. When I pause to think that out of 18,041 active pilots' licenses in the United States, only twelve are held by Negroes, and out of 8,651 mechanics' licenses only two are held by Negroes, I bow my head in shame.

Are Negroes afraid to fly? Certainly not, for we are engaged in many things far more dangerous than flying. Is it that they have not sufficient finance to learn the various branches of the aviation industry? No, that is not the case, for a thorough course in aviation engine mechanics or airplane mechanics, or even the cost of a transport pilot's course, is not nearly as much as I had to pay for my training to become a qualified electrical engineer, nor nearly as much as our boys are paying to get their training as doctors, lawyers, dentists, etc. Then what is the trouble?

After three years of aviation training and experience, I feel that I am qualified to answer this question. The answer is this:

The Negro is not aware of the various opportunities in aviation for business and employment—the fact has not been brought to his attention that the aviation industry already comprises a hundred or more branches, all of which are open to Negroes if they only qualify themselves.

MODERN PASSENGER TRANSPORT PLANE

The TWA schedule flight of this Douglas Transport from Los Angeles to New York is just over thirteen hours elapsed time.

Let us go out to the air terminal in your city where the big air transport companies have planes running on schedule time daily, to and from all points in the United States. We enter the passenger ticket office. It looks just like a railroad station in many respects. We look at the bulletin board. We note that a plane is scheduled to leave at three. Glancing through the big window we see a large tri-motored plane and a colored fellow busily engaged polishing it. The colored fellow leaves the plane as it moves up to take on the passengers. Not so bad, we think—the very first job we observed was held by a colored man, the airplane washer.

We get in line with ten or twelve people to purchase tickets from the ticket agent, the second job we observe. This gentleman is quite courteous, answering all questions as to the schedules of planes to various cities. He is white. While standing in line we notice a colored porter sweeping the floor. Another job afforded by the industry.

As we are not going very far, we have no baggage, but the people in front of us have a suit-case which is taken by a colored redcap and carried to the baggage compartment of the plane. Well, still another class of job, and a colored fellow at that. Say, that's interesting, three out of the first four jobs we observe, are held by Negroes. The person who knows no better would say immediately that the colored people are coming right along in aviation. But, alas! out of the hundreds of other types of employees in the industry, we are to see no more colored—no, not one—only the porters, redcaps, and the washers. Too bad, especially as these are the least paying jobs in the whole industry.

But we must hurry. It is almost three. We secure our tickets and hurry to the plane where a young man, usually the co-pilot of the plane, inspects our tickets just before we enter. This young man, we understand, is a limited commercial pilot who travels with the ship while building up his hours for a transport pilot's license. As we step into the large luxurious cabin of the plane we are greeted by a very pleasant young lady who seats us. This young lady is known as the hostess of the ship. She gives us cotton to put in our ears, and some chewing gum. Seeing that you are wondering why she gave you the gum, she tells you that for persons who are easily nauseated the gum settles the stomach, thus preventing nausea.

Thus, we notice employment for women already. After the young lady passes out magazines and newspapers to read, we notice a responsible-looking person step into the plane and take his place up at the front. He is the pilot. He looks back over the passengers, says a few words to the co-pilot, looks at his instruments, and then starts the motors. He taxies the plane to the far end of the field, applies the brakes, and then revs up the motors, first No. 1, then No. 2, then No. 3. Looking up in the direction in which we see him looking, we notice a man in a tower 'way up above us wave a white flag, and then we are off.

Airplane washer, redcap, porter, ticket agent, co-pilot, pilot, flagman, and hostess—eight jobs already with pay ranging in some instances from $800 per month down to $80 per month. But that's just a starter. Let us see what it takes to put that plane on the field. Let us see what it takes to prepare and maintain the field for the plane to fly to and from. Let us see if there are really opportunities in this industry for Negroes.

In reviewing these opportunities, I do not ally myself with that type of Negro who begs the white man for his job, for his opportunities; with the class of Negro leader who is constantly criticizing our white brothers because they do not give us jobs; but I do ally myself with that type of young progressive Negro who believes that a Negro has the brain, the ability, to carve out his own destiny.

Imagine, dear reader, since the transcontinental

flight is just over, that it has stirred up such enthusiasm among Negroes that they now realize that the conquest of the air is an accomplished fact. Calls are coming in from all over America from Negroes who are desirous of entering the aviation industry. They want to establish airlines operated by Negroes. They are tired of being segregated on the railroads and busses. Several prominent Negroes of Birmingham, Alabama, wish to open up an air field. They have 160 acres of ground for that purpose. But the field must be made into an AAA airport. It takes an airport engineer to supervise this job. Several Negroes are to be sent to school to be trained in airport design and construction.

They will learn how to select a suitable airport site, free from obstruction, with the prevailing winds from a suitable direction—a site which down-drafts, cross-winds, and twisters seldom frequent—they will learn to design the airport so that it will afford adequate runways to facilitate up-wind take-offs at all hours of the day and night. And, in their study of airport design and construction, they will find it necessary to call in many concrete men to lay the aprons around the hangars, as well as the concrete runways; they will find it necessary to hire brick-layers, carpenters, sheet metal workers, masons, architects, electricians, and plumbers to complete the hangars, administration buildings, offices, shops, etc., and, before the field is completed, they must call in men to install the intricate lighting system, marking the field boundary lines, with red lights denoting obstruction, green lights showing avenues of approach and runways, and white lights marking the field boundary line. The landscape gardener must not be overlooked, because the grass and shrubbery add much to the beauty of the airport. And, of course, wherever there are any business transactions, contracts, specifications, etc., to be used or made, the lawyers and stenographers come in for their share.

Think of it! All of the above trades employing many men, and only one branch of the industry so far considered! The completion of the airport at Atlanta, Georgia, calls for the construction of intermediate fields, known as emergency landing fields, between Birmingham and Atlanta. These fields are usually situated about thirty miles apart, and along this route beacons — revolving beacons, stationary beacons, blinker type beacons, and even some beacons of as high as ten million candle power, visible to flyers for 100 to 150 miles—are located, thus constituting what is known as an air line. These beacons are supplied and maintained by the government, and many more jobs are thus created in their upkeep and maintenance. Now I know my readers are surprised—so many jobs already, and the planes are not yet manufactured.

With the shops and factories already built, we now observe several Negroes, aeronautical engineers, who have successfully qualified, designing planes. Some are designing fast planes, others, planes that will carry a heavy load. They learn that the wing curves of a fast plane are quite different from those of a plane designed to have a greater lift, that is, a plane that will carry a heavier load. They also learn that they must sacrifice a large pay load to get speed, and that speed must be sacrified to get a greater weight-carrying capacity. They learn that the greater the streamline of the various parts of the plane, the less the wind resistance, and hence the faster the plane. And that the shape of the "camber" (wing curve) of the wing determines the amount of lift. They learn likewise that various arrangements of dihedral, wing stagger, decalage, angle of incidence, wing gap, etc., give varying degrees of stability, and that the propeller screws through the air, pulling the ship after it, just as a screw of a boat churns through the water, pushing the boat along. Educated men, those aeronautical engineers!—They must know mathematics, chemistry, physics—plenty of each—and it seems that they speak a different language from that of the ordinary person, for all one hears when around them are such terms as "aspect ratio," "lift-drag ratio," "washout and washin," "slenderness ratio," "normal flight," "lateral and longitudinal stability," "positive tail," "sweepback," "keel area," "parasite resistance," "wing loading," and "biplane efficiency". But these are the highest paid men in the whole industry.

From the design room we go to the drafting room where mechanical draftsmen are recording the ideas of the aeronautical engineers. We see a colored blue-printer emerge with an arm full of blue-prints, carrying them to the colored airplane mechanics who are skilled in the building of wings, tail surfaces, ailerons, stabilizers, etc., placing the wing spars, leading edge, ribs, etc., in place as only a well-trained Negro can do. In another department, we see the fuselage taking shape. While in another room colored girls are seen stitching fabric on the wings and the fuselage. We are choked somewhat by fumes as we enter the dope room where Negro men are smearing several coats of dope on the wings, fuselage, and tail empennage.

In still another department, men are assembling the various parts of the airplane, which is now ready for the engine mechanics to mount the motor and propeller. The skilled sign painters put on the plane the large numerals and letters which are required by the Department of Commerce for identification.

When the plane is completely assembled and the motor run in for several hours and all instruments installed, we see a colored man with a parachute on getting into the plane to "put it through the works". After many power dives, tail spins, loops, rolls, and every conceivable stunt, the plane is pronounced O.K. by this test pilot—a job that pays an enormous salary.

And so we see many jobs awaiting us, and others too numerous to mention. The ship is now ready for the pilot. Yes, I know you are more than surprised, for when you think of aviation, you think only of the pilot and mechanic—you do not realize that it takes hundreds of other trades and professions to make it possible for the pilot and mechanic to function.

And then, too, most of you think that all a pilot must learn is how to manipulate the controls to fly the ship. Again you are quite wrong. In fact, one never becomes a competent pilot until he learns aeronautics, navigation, meteorology, and mechanics.

In his study of aerodynamics, or air flow about surfaces, the pilot learns what makes an aeroplane fly. In his study of navigation, he learns how to go from city to city without getting lost. In his study of meteorology, he learns the various cloud formations and what kind of weather to expect. His mechanical training teaches him how to inspect his motor and keep it in proper running condition, and how to inspect his airplane and keep it in the proper state of repair. To learn all these things then, we need a host of Negro teachers, both men and women. Another important branch of the aviation industry is the radio department. Radio operators are now being carried on all long flights, and most airplanes are now installing radio sets to pick up weather reports.

Hence we see that with the proper co-operation, interest, and enthusiasm, a gigantic industry among Negroes would soon spring up, giving hundreds of thousands of jobs to the unemployed. The millions of dollars that Negroes pay the railroads and busses annually would be diverted back into their own pockets.

Airplane manufacturers would spring up with colored distributing agencies, colored finance companies, and, of course, what would follow these would be colored businesses for repossessed airplanes, and sales of second-hand planes.

And then, passenger transport business is not the

only outlet for development in aviation. Freight and express by air are coming factors.

Do you know that the mystery of bird flying has been solved by a black inventor?

Floyd C. Covington, Executive Secretary of the Los Angeles Urban League, met this inventor, and gives us a wonderful description of the secrets of the Vortex Wing invented by this Negro, Mr. Jay Howard Montgomery.

He relates how Montgomery analyzed 20,000 specimens of dead birds, and made hundreds of microscopic studies of every detail of the wing construction, and finally concluded that Nature had built a power house within their wings. Developing a special means of preserving dead birds in a rigid flying position, he sent them aloft by toy balloons. One travelled more than twelve miles from an altitude of 1,500 feet. From his investigations he deduced that the wing of a vulture as a whole is an airfoil—a lifting surface, but that it is an airfoil in three directions: from the shoulder to the tip in length, from the shoulder to the tip in a twist on a 45-degree angle, and in cross-section; that each of the twenty-three feathers is made up of three airfoils, or feathers within feathers. He found that the air striking the wing starts spiraling, creating minute vacuums, finally being whirled off the rear of the tail, as well as toward the wing tip of the body. Montgomery found that the combined effect of the tiny vacuums is a forward thrust, and is the explanation of how such a winged body can create its own forward power within the wing itself.

The vultured-wing plane, according to the inventor, could, having gained altitude, shut off its motor and soar around the world without again turning it on. It could land or take off in any small area, office buildings included, as it requires only sixty feet for runway.

If it should develop, as is now believed by many scientists and technical experts who have seen the model perform, that the black inventor has solved the mystery of bird flying, then massed flapping of Black Wings is only a question of time.

Airplanes will some day bring the green vegetables of the distant farmer within a few minutes of his market, and these vegetables will not have to be crated and iced in order to reach the city fresh, but will be picked, loaded into an airplane, and delivered to the market in the city within a few hours.

Fruits that now have to be shipped green via railroad to keep from spoiling will hang on the tree and reach proper size, flavor, and maturity before being shipped via air. "Flowers by wire" will become flowers by air.

Aero-dusting is developing rapidly, and is now being carried on commercially in many countries. Not longer than nine years ago, a pair of progressive and enthusiastic entomologists undertook to demonstrate to the more conservative and generally skeptical members of their profession, the practicability of employing aircraft as a means of distributing insecticides over otherwise inaccessible areas of trees. Their experiment was a signal success. It represented the most revolutionary development in man's age-old warfare against his insect enemies that the world had witnessed.

This method has been used to distribute various insecticides in dust form to control the Catalpa sphinx moth, gipsy moth, hemlock spanworm, pecan case borer, sugar cane borer, cotton boll weevil, coddling moth on apple trees, aphis infesting prune, walnut, and other trees, grasshoppers, cucumber beetles, army worms in lima beans, alfalfa weevil, leaf hoppers on beets, cotton leaf worms, citrus thrips, various species of spider mites on almonds, cherries, citrus, figs, peaches, prunes, and walnuts, and other pests on cranberries and vegetables.

Among plant diseases that this modern method of

applying fungicides in dust form has been used to control are: peach and prune brown rot, pecan scab, powdery mildew of grapes, red and alsike clover, apple scab, and leaf and stem rust of cereals.

The grape acreage in California dusted by airplane with sulphur dust to control powdery mildew has been considerable, and preceded the work in orchards. From the standpoint of commercial acreage involved, California has within the past two years submitted an imposing total of fruit trees to aero-dusting treatment. Almonds, citrus, figs, peaches, prunes, walnuts, have been aero-dusted for red spiders; lemons for thrips; prunes and walnuts for aphis. The predominating pests involved to date have been spider mites, and the bulk of tonnage of insecticides used has been sulphur dust.

On May 1, 1925, W. J. Chamberlin, Assistant Entomologist at the Oregon Experimenting Station, assisted by Lieut. O. G. Kelly, Pilot in the U. S. Air Service, applied a mixture of lead arsenate and sulphur to a portion of the Oregon A. C. orchards at Monroe, Oregon. The application was made to control apple scab and coddling moth, and a partial comparison of ground and aerial dusting effected. The vital conclusions drawn were that aero-dusting was commercially possible; large areas could be covered rapidly and effectively with no more material per acre than commonly used with ground equipment.

I saw my first aero-dusting operation at Bakersfield, California. An Eagle Rock biplane equipped with a 150 H.P. Hispano Suiza motor, and equipped with the standard dusting hopper adapted from specifications furnished by the United States Department of Agriculture, was dusting 150 acres of prunes. After watching these operations both from the ground and from the air, I engaged in conversation with the pilot of the aero-dusting plane.

I learned that this plane was capable of carrying

1,000 pounds of dusting material and delivered any desired poundage per acre while traveling at a speed of 125 miles per hour. The average poundage per acre spread over this particular field was fifty pounds, applied at a rate to the grower of $1.50 per acre. The amazing thing was that a speed of application of as high as twenty-five acres per minute was obtainable with that plane.

Further investigation into the aero-dusting activities of airplanes disclosed many interesting facts that every farmer, white or black, should know.

The advantages of aero-dusting are:

1. Speed of application; 2. thoroughness of coverage; 3. conservation of dusting material; 4. saving in time, labor, and investment in other equipment; 5. independence of, and non-interference with, other orchard practices; 6. the possibility of treating non-orchard tracts, that border on cultivated areas and which harbor insects or diseases; 7. the possibility of community effort in wholesale control of epidemics of insects or diseases, which may catch the orchardist unprepared to combat them; and, 8. nominal cost per acre for the service.

There is a possibility of aero-dusting for control of any disease or insect that can be controlled by insecticides or fungicides in dust form—and soon the presence of aero-dusting aircraft will be as commonplace over orchards and fields as "yellow jackets over a cider barrel".

The airplane in agriculture is not confined to crop pest and disease control—it is employed in forest fire and other patrol work; in making crop surveys and estimates; in eradicating malarial mosquitoes and scouting for possible breeding places; in scouting for outlaw cotton fields; in collecting air borne rust spores; in tripping legume blossoms; in spreading fertilizers; in seeding large areas to rice, pasture, and range grasses.

Are Negro farmers preparing for these aerial activities which will affect the market price of their crops considerably? Are the Negro farmers training their youth to take up these thousands of jobs which will soon be created by airplanes in agriculture? Will the Negro farmer continue to germicide, plant, and seed his crops and fruit by the old hand method after the white farmers are using the air methods? If so he will be as far behind the white farmers as the farmer who uses an ox team is behind the one who uses a tractor. And, dear readers, do you realize that the farmer who does not keep up with these advance methods of farming will not be able to market his goods as cheaply as the other farmer?

Once I happened upon a little fishing village on the bay of Lower California in Old Mexico. This village exports thousands of pounds of fish daily to the markets in San Pedro, California. Hundreds of Mexicans were engaged in the business of transporting this fish to San Pedro by trucks. Thousands of dollars were invested in large trucks, costly trucks, as the roads in Mexico over which they had to travel are terrible. It would take several hours to load the fish in the truck since it had to be iced, as the journey by road required three or four and sometimes five days. Ofttimes the drivers had to stop en route to San Pedro and again ice the load of fish.

Upon noticing this condition I thought: Now if we only had about fifty Negro transport pilots, and if a few Negro financiers could be approached and interested, we could put several airplanes hauling fish between this little fishing village and San Pedro at a great saving, thus enabling us to market the fish much lower than the present market price, because the time saved would permit us to dispense with the use of ice entirely. The trip which would ordinarily require four days could easily be made in four hours and instead of using a thousand pounds of ice to each ton of fish the load would only be one ton.

I had occasion to make friends with one of the Mexican trucksters who lived in Calexico. Six months later while stopping in Calexico, I visited this Mexican friend and found him to be in a very destitute condition. He was not long in telling me that the Apache Air Lines had put several airplanes on the line carrying fish to San Pedro so cheaply that the fellows driving trucks could not operate—and a similar fate awaits the Negro farmer if he does not keep up with improvements that are creeping upon him daily.

And yet we still cry for jobs—for opportunities— when they are all around us! Again I say, we, our business leaders, our financial leaders, are sound asleep. Taking into consideration the fact that there are large numbers of farms owned and operated by Negroes throughout America, then agricultural aviation opens a field of thousands of jobs for Negroes—good paying jobs.

Fighting forest fires has become quite a business for the airplane. Air police and air patrols along the borders are becoming more and more necessary each day. Aerial photography is playing a great part in the real estate business today, and there are many, many other things that can and will be done by the airplane.

Many intelligent, educated Negroes do not have the slightest conception of the aviation industry. One Sunday, Rev. Addison, a very well educated minister, visited my church, Beth Eden Baptist Church in Los Angeles.

My mother was introduced to him as the mother of Lieut. Powell, the aviator, who sings in the choir.

"Lieut. Powell?" replied the minister, astonished. However, he said no more.

At the close of church services when our pastor, Rev. Eldridge, introduced the visiting minister to the congregation, in the course of his remarks, the Rev. Addison said, "I'm most surprised to know that Lieut. Powell, the aviator, sings in the choir here. I thought all aviators were sports and I never expected to see one singing in a church choir."

And so it is with thousands of other Negroes, intelligent Negroes at that; they are ignorant of the facts concerning an industry which bids fair to rival all other great industries—they merely think of aviation as a sporting pastime.

Are not these facts conclusive evidence that wonderful opportunities await the Negro in aviation if he will only act? Negro leaders—why do you sleep? Black men and black women—arouse your imaginations. Act before it is too late. Do not let the aviation industry become completely monopolized and built up by other races who will only give you and me the most menial jobs of porter, redcap, and washer; but get into aviation now while we have a chance to have black airplane manufacturers, black airplane designers, black airplane distributors, owners of black air transport lines, and have thousands of black boys and black girls profitably employed in a great paying industry.

Do you know the story of the Goldbergs and Silversteins? No? Every Negro mother should tell this story to her children. Only a few years ago, the Jews were disliked and segregated on all sides by their white brethren in America. Jews were denied rooms in the fashionable hotels of the large cities. They were refused the best theatre boxes. I even recall the time when I was a student at the Wendell Phillips High School in Chicago, when the Jewish boys and girls were segregated and were more disliked than were we colored fellows.

But, did the Jews send up great cries to the white men that they were being segregated, ostracized from society, etc? A thousand times, no! Instead, Jews pooled their money, and went into business. Jewish women pulled off their rings and diamonds and pooled them for finance to open business. Jews hired Jews. Jews patronized Jews, and in a marvelously short time Jews built finer and better hotels and theatres than those from which they had been excluded and the result is, today, Jews are no longer segregated, because they control the money markets. They control some of the largest industries of the day. You can't segregate a Jew in a theatre today because the Jews control the motion picture industry and the show business. That is the story of the Goldbergs and Silversteins.

Negro leaders, will there be an interesting story to relate to the young ones in the days to come about filling the air with "Black Wings"?

CHAPTER XIV

A PLAN

IF THERE IS THE PROPER INTEREST, EN-
THUSIASM, and CO-OPERATION;
and

IF WE HAVE THE TRAINED MEN AND
WOMEN AS TEACHERS;
and

IF WE HAVE FACTORIES, SHOPS, FIELDS,
AND PLANES;
and

IF WE HAVE SUFFICIENT FINANCE;
then

we can get all these things that we have found so
desirable.

So, dear readers, I submit my plan, although I feel
that we have leaders in and out of business far more
competent than I to suggest, and therefore I only offer
this as a basis or suggestion to start with; the details
to be worked out as necessary.

First, WE HAVE LEADERS CAPABLE OF
STIRRING UP INTEREST IN ANYTHING IF THEY
WOULD ONLY DO SO; leaders whom, whatever they
decide is best for the rest of us, the majority will follow; who can sway the public at will. I have refer-
ence to our ministers, our editors, the leaders of our
fraternal organizations.

Therefore we will select the leading Negro editors,
the religious leaders of our race, and the leaders of the
fraternal organizations, and form a committee in trust.
This committee will supervise a campaign in which
each town or city in America having a Negro population of importance will sponsor one or more young

men and women, sending them to a school of aeronautics to be established in Los Angeles (because one can fly the year 'round in Los Angeles).

This school in Los Angeles shall be supervised by Negroes but taught, at the beginning, in most part, by white instructors.

A period of one year would be allotted each city to raise its funds to pay for the cost of training its students and their upkeep. These funds might be raised by giving a series of affairs or events, or by voluntary taxing of all Negro affairs given during the year five or ten per cent. At the end of the year the money would be forwarded to the committee, or better, in quarterly periods, to enable the committee to prepare the school and facilities, make its budget, and attend to other necessary details.

Each city would pay the regular cost per person for aviation training. The money sent to train from three to four hundred students would be sufficient to give them a course of training equal to, and probably better than, that which the average school offers for the same price, and then have sufficient left to build the school, field, etc., and purchase equipment, providing the school is operated on a NON-PROFIT BASIS.

The students at this school would be selected by competitive examination after the money had been raised in each city. Some cities might send one, some two, some three or even more. It would take one year, average, to train the first quota.

The highest standing students at the end of the term would be selected as teachers and assistant teachers at the school, which would also get a large number of other students not eligible to be sponsored, for there are thousands of young Negro boys and girls now desiring a place in which to obtain aviation training. Other students qualifying would be sent back to their respective cities where they would engage in carrying passengers off their field in their own city—short pleasure trips—this would make the masses air-minded. Later these same pilots would carry passengers from their town to the next, and finally an air line would be established.

The best students in the design room would be retained and hired by the school to design a plane, or planes, which the students would build or experiment with. As soon as perfected, students qualifying would be retained to build the first plane, and then more planes. Others would be sent out as agents to sell the planes, and eventually Negroes would be purchasing planes designed and built by Negroes. And so the industry would progress, and a field could be maintained in each city by its colored population. Within a few years a gigantic industry could be built up by Negroes.

The white race is taking up flying by leaps and bounds. Do you know that in 1931, 38,774 people took the medical examination to become airplane pilots? Do you know that there are 816 medical examiners employed by the United States Department of Commerce and NOT ONE COLORED?

And yet, in common with all other industries, the aviation industry is suffering from depressing influences. Doubtless, in some respects, it has felt these influences more keenly than most others. It is comparatively new and was not so deeply rooted, nor did it have the background of organized experience. Also, at the beginning of this period of economic unrest the industry as a whole had been promoted beyond any reasonable premise of development. It had a great distance from which to recede, and the recession was both painful and exacting. Times changed suddenly, and the industry found itself confronted with the necessity of revising its plans and ideas along economic lines more nearly suited to the changed conditions.

To arrive at a suitable premise, perhaps it would be in order to recall the beginnings of the present aeronautic industry and to review briefly its accomplishments to date.

We all know that flying, as now constituted, dates from 1903 when the Wright brothers made their successful flights at Kitty Hawk; that the ensuing development of consequence was during the World War, and that there took place thereafter the post-war period of flying, using surplus war material, which paved the way for the first real efforts at commercial flying.

However, I wonder if we all retain in mind the fact that it was but six or seven years ago, approximately, that there was any real organized and comprehensive effort to develop civil aeronautics, and but some four and a half years ago that scheduled operations with transportation of mail were undertaken by private enterprise, and only little more than two years since similar effort was devoted to scheduled transportation of passengers.

In 1931 airplanes flew in regularly scheduled service over 47,000,000 miles. They transported 522,000 passengers and 10,000,000 pounds of mail.

Also in the last five-year period, or during the existence of the Aeronautics Branch of the Department of Commerce, an airway system has been constructed in the United States, the like of which exists in no other country in the world. It is made up of all known aids to navigation, and constitutes at present a 19,500 mile highway system of the air.

In the last three years, the period when all industry has been adversely affected by economic conditions, air transportation has shown a remarkable progress. As a matter of fact, this progress seems to be one of the outstanding accomplishments of commerce and industry during this period. The airplane mileage flown increased from 25,000,000 in 1929 to 47,000,000 in 1931; the number of passengers transported by scheduled services increased from 173,000 in 1929 to 522,000 in 1931; and air mail from 7,770,000 pounds to 9,640,-000 pounds.

Even so, the Negro has a chance to get in on the ground floor yet; but he will have to act now, if he hopes to fill the air with "Black Wings".

APPENDIX

A list of Negroes in the United States holding licenses December 31, 1932, is herewith presented through the courtesy of Congressman Oscar Depriest and is compiled from records of the United States Department of Commerce.

TRANSPORT LICENSE
C. Alfred Anderson..............Bryn Mawr, Pennsylvania
License No. 7638

LIMITED COMMERCIAL LICENSE
John W. Green...............................Boston, Massachusetts
License No. 15,897

INDUSTRIAL LICENSE
Mrs. Jany Harmon Waterford....................Chicago, Ill.
License No. 7934

PRIVATE LICENSE
James Herman Banning (Deceased)..Los Angeles, Cal.
License No. 1324

Leon Parrish ....New York City
License No. 16,069

Hubert Julian ....New York City
License No. 21,512

Lincoln Payne...................................Philadelphia, Pa.
License No. 23,575

William J. Powell...............................Los Angeles, Cal.
License No. 24,335

James Hoard....................................San Francisco, Cal.
License No. 26,035

John C. Robinson....................................Chicago, Illinois
License No. 26,042

Cecil O'Neal..New York City
License No. 27,179
Pickens Black...Jackson County, Ark.
License No. 27,677
Dr. Albert E. Forsythe.....................Atlantic City, N. J.
License No. 27,287
Dr. C. C. (Jack) Petitt..............................New York City

LICENSED MECHANICS

John W. Green..............................Boston, Massachusetts
Mechanics License No. 10,658
Cornelius Coffey...Chicago, Illinois
Mechanics License No. 11,598

CERTIFIED PARACHUTE RIGGER

Ed Smith..Cincinnati, Ohio

NAVIGATOR (AVIGATOR)

William J. Powell..Los Angeles, Cal.
Irvin E. Wells ....Los Angeles, Cal.

AERONAUTICAL ENGINEERS

Jay Howard Montgomery ....Los Angeles, Cal.
William J. Powell ....Los Angeles, Cal.

A transport pilot's license is the highest type of flying license granted by the Department of Commerce. A transport pilot may pilot any type of licensed airplane and may carry persons for hire in licensed conventional types of airplanes within the classes specified in their licenses. They may also teach students *for hire*.

A limited commercial pilot may pilot all types of licensed airplanes but may not instruct students *for hire* nor carry persons *for hire* outside of the areas mentioned in his license.

Industrial pilots may pilot any type of licensed aircraft not carrying persons *for hire*. He shall not instruct students *for hire*. This class of license has recently been discontinued by the Department of Commerce.

Private pilots may pilot any type of licensed aircraft but may not carry passengers *for hire* nor instruct students *for hire*.

Student pilots are licensed only for the purpose of piloting licensed aircraft when receiving flying instructions. They may not go beyond a safe gliding distance from the field on which they are receiving instruction.

There are several good pilots, however, holding only a private pilot's license, and some with only a student's permit. Reasons for this are obvious; for in order to maintain a transport pilot's license or a limited commercial license, one must pay for a physical examination every six months, as well as fly at least ten hours every six months, all of which costs a considerable sum of money if one is not commercially engaged in flying. On the other hand, to maintain a private pilot's license, one must pay for only one physical examination per year and for only ten hours of flying per year. Hence, many good pilots not commercially engaged in flying prefer to keep only a private pilot's license in order to cut down expense.

This explains why James Herman Banning held only a private license at the time of his passing, notwithstanding the fact he had held a limited commercial license twice.